500 RECIPES FOR DINNERS & SUPPER PARTIES

by Marguerite Patten

HAMLYN

LONDON · NEW YORK · SYDNEY · TORONTO

Contents

Cover photograph by courtesy of The House of Hallgarten, Shippers of fine wines, spirits and liqueurs.

Liebfraumilch Kellergeist from S.F. & O. Hallgarten
Santos Rosé from L. Rosenheim & Sons Ltd.
Royal Mint Chocolate Liqueur from Maurice Meyer Ltd.
Hibachi home barbecue from Le Creuset Vitrified
Cast-Ironware by courtesy of Clarbat Ltd., London
Photographed by Angel Studios.

The picture shows Parma ham and figs (see page 24),
Barbecue chicken (see page 71), Barbecue sauce (see
page 73), Green salad (see page 52), Potatoes tossed
in butter and chopped parsley, Walnut pie (see page 21).

Introduction	3
Some Useful Facts and Figures	3
To Keep Food Hot	5
To Keep Food Looking Fresh	5
To Keep Costs Down	7
Dinner Parties	8
Supper Parties	42
Teenage Supper Parties	64
Menus With At Least One Hot Dish	71
Bring It With You Menus	75
Tray Suppers	77
One Dish Supper Parties	78
When the Family Takes Over	79
After Theatre Supper Parties	82
Choosing Wines	86
Setting the Table	88
Store Cupboard Menus	88
Index	94

Published by
THE HAMLYN PUBLISHING GROUP LIMITED
LONDON · NEW YORK · SYDNEY · TORONTO
Hamlyn House, Feltham, Middlesex, England

© Copyright Marguerite Patten 1966
ISBN 0 600 32846 5
Revised edition 1971

Printed in England by Cox and Wyman Ltd,
London, Reading and Fakenham

Introduction

So often in my post bag I have requests from people, many who are experienced and accomplished housewives, who wish for new ideas for those occasions when they entertain friends and acquaintances. It seemed to me, therefore, that the most helpful way to give you these recipes was in the form of suggested menus.

Planning a menu for other people is not easy, for personal likes and dislikes are normally considered, but I have tried to give the sort of menu that is easy for the hostess to prepare when she has little, if any, help; if there are unexpected problems I have mentioned them in the menu.

Servings may sometimes seem a little inexplic-able. For example, the main dish will serve 4, but the sweet has been given to serve 4–6. This is because most of us like to have a little extra to offer as a second helping. In some menus, particularly for buffet parties, you have a rather wide range of dishes. You may not wish to make all these. That is why the servings at the top of each recipe are given to cover ample amounts for a certain number of people. If, however, you are making the entire menu, a dish which will give 4 ample portions if served by itself, will serve 8 or even 10 people if they are having a wide variety.

I hope you enjoy this book, and that it will enable you to entertain with pleasure and confidence.

Some Useful Facts and Figures

Comparison of Weights and Measures

English weights and measures have been used throughout the book. 3 teaspoonfuls equal 1 tablespoon. The average English teacup is $\frac{1}{4}$ pint. The average English breakfast cup is $\frac{1}{2}$ pint. When cups are mentioned in recipes they refer to a B.S.I. measuring cup which holds $\frac{1}{2}$ pint or 10 fluid ounces. In case it is wished to translate quantities into American or metric counterparts the following give a comparison.

Liquid measure

The American pint is 16 fluid ounces, as opposed to the British Imperial pint and Canadian pint which are 20 fluid ounces. The American $\frac{1}{2}$-pint measuring cup is therefore equivalent to $\frac{2}{5}$ British pint. In Australia the British Imperial pint, 20 fluid ounces, is used.

Solid measure

British	American
1 lb. butter or other fat	2 cups
1 lb. flour	4 cups
1 lb. granulated or castor sugar	2 cups
1 lb. icing or confectioners' sugar	3 cups

British	American
1 lb. brown (moist) sugar	$2\frac{1}{2}$ cups
1 lb. golden syrup or treacle	1 cups
1 lb. rice	2 cups
1 lb. dried fruit	2 cups
1 lb. chopped meat (finely packed)	2 cups
1 lb. lentils or split peas	2 cups
1 lb. coffee (unground)	$2\frac{1}{4}$ cups
1 lb. soft breadcrumbs	4 cups
$\frac{1}{2}$ oz. flour	1 level tablespoon
1 oz. flour	1 heaped tablespoon
1 oz. sugar	1 level tablespoon
$\frac{1}{2}$ oz. butter	1 level tablespoon smoothed off
1 oz. golden syrup or treacle	1 level tablespoon
1 oz. jam or jelly	1 level tablespoon

All U.S. standard measuring tablespoons

To help you understand metrication

You will see from the chart that 1 oz. is approximately 28 grammes but can be rounded off to the more convenient measuring unit of 25. Also the figures in the right hand column are not always increased by 25. This is to reduce the difference between the convenient number and the nearest equivalent. If in a recipe the ingredients to be converted are 1 oz. of margarine and 6 oz. of flour, these are the conversions: 25 grammes margarine and 175 grammes flour.

The conversion chart

Ounces	Approx. g and ml to nearest whole number	Approx. to nearest unit of 25
1	28	25
2	57	50
3	85	75
4	113	125
5	142	150
6	170	175
7	198	200
8	226	225
12	340	350
16	456	450

Note: When converting quantities over 16 oz. first add the appropriate figures in the centre column, not those given in the right hand column, THEN adjust to the nearest unit of 25 grammes. For example, to convert $1\frac{3}{4}$ lb. add 456 to 340 grammes which equals 796 grammes. When rounded off to the convenient figure it becomes 800 grammes.

Approximate liquid conversions

$\frac{1}{4}$ pint–150 ml   *1,000 millilitres–1 1 (litre)
$\frac{1}{2}$ pint–275 ml   1 litre–$1\frac{3}{4}$ pints
$\frac{3}{4}$ pint–425 ml $\frac{1}{2}$ litre–$\frac{3}{4}$ pint plus 4 tablespoons
1 pint–575 ml   1 dl (decilitre)–6 tablespoons

Note: If solid ingredients give scant weight using the 25 unit conversion, the amount of liquid allowed must also be scant. For example, although 575 ml is nearer to 1 pint (20 fluid oz.) when making a white pouring sauce use 550 ml of milk to 25 grammes each of butter and flour for a better consistency.

Oven Temperatures

The following chart gives conversions from degrees Fahrenheit to degrees Celsius (formerly known as Centigrade). This chart is accurate to within 3° Celsius, and can therefore be used for recipes which give oven temperatures in metric.

Note: This table is an approximate guide only. Different makes of cooker vary and if you are in any doubt about the setting it is as well to refer to the manufacturer's temperature chart.

Description	Electric Setting	Gas Mark
VERY COOL	225°F–110°C	$\frac{1}{4}$
	250°F–130°C	$\frac{1}{2}$
COOL	275°F–140°C	1
	300°F–150°C	2
MODERATE	325°F–170°C	3
	350°F–180°C	4
MODERATELY HOT	375°F–190°C	5
	400°F–200°C	6
HOT	425°F–220°C	7
	450°F–230°C	8
VERY HOT	475°F–240°C	9

To Keep Food Hot

One of the most difficult tasks is to keep food hot without it becoming overcooked and dry. When you are entertaining and a meal is ready to dish up, it does help enormously if the food can be dished up some little time before your guests arrive so that there is no last minute 'panic'. There are a number of ways in which the food can be kept without spoiling.

If the oven heat is turned to its very lowest, food can be kept in this, but do put pieces of foil or greaseproof paper over the top so it does not dry. Allow a very generous amount of margarine or butter when tossing the vegetables.

If your oven is still being used for cooking, then food should be kept hot over pans of hot, but not boiling, water. If the water boils rapidly it will continue to cook the food.

Your vegetable dishes may fit comfortably on the top of the saucepan, or stand over a plate on the top of the saucepan. Here again keep them well covered so they do not dry.

If you do a great deal of entertaining it is well worth while investing in a hot plate or some form of food warmer. There are various types on the market, many of them elegant enough to be in use in the dining-room. So the moment the food is ready you can dish it up, keep it warm, and get as much of the washing up as possible out of the way.

To keep sauces hot

Sauces, which need a fair amount of attention, can be made in the top of a double saucepan earlier in the day, then re-heated gently over hot water. This saves the problem of the sauce sticking if left unattended for a time.

Any sauce, whether sweet or savoury, containing flour or cornflour, forms a skin if it is kept standing. To avoid this, put a piece of foil or greaseproof paper under the cold tap, shake fairly dry, press the damp paper or foil immediately on top of the sauce after it is cooked – do not give it a chance to cool before doing this.

Custard and sauces can be transferred to serving jugs when made, covered as above, then re-heated by standing in a saucepan of water, which is brought gradually to the boil. Gravies can be prepared in the same way.

To keep meat and poultry hot

The easiest thing to do is to transfer meat or poultry on to a hot serving dish and put into the oven, which should be turned down very low. Keep covered with foil to prevent drying. If carving beforehand, do keep the slices well covered, since nothing looks more unappetising then dry meat or poultry.

To Keep Food Looking Fresh

Even the plainest food will look exciting if it is fresh, and when you have to make a lot of preparations in advance it is quite difficult to make sure that salads look crisp and green, cocktail savouries do not dry on top, that bread and butter or sandwiches will not curl at the edges.

Fortunately today there is a very wide selection of kitchen papers which do keep food fresh for a very long time. Cover bread and butter, sandwiches and cakes either with aluminium foil, with polythene (i.e. the transparent wrapping), or with paper from a roll of kitchen paper. In the case of the latter, sandwiches and bread and butter should be covered with slightly dampened paper to keep them really fresh for a long time.

Because the polythene wrapping is so light in weight this is probably the best covering for cocktail savouries, as it does not rest on the food. Foil can also be lifted slightly so that it is tucked in firmly round the edge of the dish while forming a 'dome' over the top of the food. Salads, once arranged, keep perfectly under polythene or foil, or damp kitchen paper. They can be placed in the refrigerator, but even there it is absolutely imperative that they are wrapped. Dishes and plates of cold meat keep better wrapped as above, rather than having a second plate or dish put over the top.

Cream piped on the top of sweets will harden and dry in the air unless you cover them. Here foil is better because it is stiff enough to raise well above the dish so that it cannot possibly fall on to the sweet and harm the decoration. When you wish to keep cold drinks cold, without a refrigerator, remember that vacuum flasks do this very satisfactorily, in exactly the same way that they keep hot drinks hot for a considerable period.

To Keep Costs Down

Often people wrongly imagine that in order to entertain you must have very expensive dishes. This is quite wrong. The simplest foods, if attractively and originally presented, can be served to guests as well as to the family. That is why in this book you will find recipes using sausages, liver and stewing steak, but they produce results which most people will thoroughly enjoy. Very often you can have a quite cheap dish turned into something exotic by an interesting sauce. Many of the sweets need cream, and it is possible to save money by using one of the mock creams from the recipes given.

Mock creams with a cream maker

you will need for a thin cream:
½ pint milk
8 oz. unsalted margarine or butter
flavouring and sweetening to taste

For a thick cream:*
¼ pint milk
8 oz. unsalted margarine or butter
flavouring and sweetening to taste

*A thick cream will hold a soft shape when piped.

1 Heat the milk and butter or margarine to blood heat only and then allow to cool.
2 Put through the cream maker.
3 If a very thick cream is wanted, use the second recipe and put through twice.
4 The sugar and flavouring can be added after the cream is made.
5 Suitable to serve with sweets, to add to cold mixtures, but never to be put into a hot mixture.

Evaporated milk cream

1 Boil a can of evaporated milk for 15 minutes.
2 Open carefully and pour into a bowl.
3 Cool for several hours and whip.
4 For a stiffer cream, dissolve 1 teaspoon powdered gelatine in 1–2 tablespoons of very hot water, add to a medium-sized can evaporated milk after boiling, and proceed as above.
5 Use to serve in a sweet, as a decoration, although it will not pipe, or to add to cold mixtures.

Butter cream

you will need:
2 oz. butter, preferably unsalted
2 oz. sleved icing sugar
1–2 tablespoons milk

1 Cream the butter and sugar until very soft and light.
2 Gradually beat in the milk.
3 Suitable for filling gateaux, as decoration, ideal for piping.

To make cream lighter

After a fairly elaborate meal, ordinary cream can sometimes be too rich.
Lighter creams are made as follows:

Method 1
¼ pint thick cream
1 egg white
little sugar to taste, preferably icing sugar

1 Whip the cream until stiff enough to hold its shape.
2 Whisk the egg white in a separate bowl until very stiff, fold in the sugar, then fold this carefully into the cream. The mixture will pipe and keep its shape.

Method 2
1 If using very thick cream, whip until it just holds its shape.
2 Add a little vanilla essence and sugar if wished, then gradually and gently stir in milk, which gives a much less heavy solid cream.

Dinner Parties

To plan dinner parties

To plan a dinner party may sound rather frightening to an inexperienced cook and hostess. In fact, it is one of the easiest ways of entertaining, providing you are sensible in your choice of menu.

1 If you have to work unaided, do plan those foods that can be prepared well beforehand, will not spoil if left in the oven a little longer than you anticipate – for nothing is worse than to hurry one's guests or be on tenterhooks because food may be ruined by 10 minutes extra pleasant chat.

2 Do not attempt ambitious dishes that you have never tried before, unless you are very sure of your cooking ability.

3 Rather choose the type of food you know you cook beautifully, and dress it up by extra special garnishes or accompaniments.

4 The menus in this section are only chosen for a relatively small number of guests. Obviously if you have a large dinner party you double or treble the ingredients. It is rather better to have a smaller number of people who can receive your personal attention.

5 Immediately following you will find some suggestions for cocktail savouries to serve to your guests when they first arrive. When you are entertaining them to a complete meal there is no need to serve very substantial cocktail savouries, unless you mean these to take the place of a first course. This is often a very good idea, if your main course is better served very freshly cooked.

6 At the beginning of the book you will find hints on keeping food hot, and if you can dish up before your guests are due, it does mean a much more leisurely atmosphere for you.

Little mention has been made of the vegetables to serve with the main dish. This is because it will vary according to the time of year. Try to have vegetables that complement the main dish:

(a) in texture – if this is very soft and creamy then crispy potatoes and firm textured vegetables like cauliflowers or beans, are a wise choice.

(b) in colour – if the dish is pale, then you need bright colourful vegetables; if very vivid, then green vegetables generally blend well.

Remember that the modern tendency is to serve salads with hot dishes, and these can save a lot of last minute cooking and dishing up and be the perfect partner to roasts and grills.

The food you serve

The first course

Unless it is to be a very formal dinner party, most people are satisfied with three courses, plus perhaps cheese and fresh fruit. Your choice of first course depends entirely on the main dish. If this is substantial and very filling, then fruit in the form of melon, grapefruit or fruit juices would be adequate. Or choose a light fish course such as smoked salmon, trout, a prawn cocktail or salad. If the main course is to be cold, then a light hot first course is ideal.

The main dish

If you have experienced help in the kitchen, then grilled steaks and fried foods are ideal. If you have to work unaided this will mean that you, as the hostess, must leave your guests for some little time before the meal is served. If they are old friends, this will not matter.

Roast meats and poultry are general favourites. There will be delay in carving, but providing you or the man of the house is a quick, accomplished carver this will not matter. If you dislike carving, either try to joint your meat or carve it, and keep hot on a dish covered with foil before the guests arrive, or choose another type of main dish.

Casserole foods are of course an ideal choice. They do not spoil with a little extra cooking. The entire dish and sauce is prepared beforehand, so there is no last minute cooking. Many of the modern ceramic and other ovenware casseroles are attractive enough to put on the table, so the food goes straight from the oven to be served, piping hot. Do not imagine that a casserole is dull. By a wise choice of wine, interesting herbs and vegetables, it can be a really exciting dish.

The sweet

There is such an infinite variety of sweets from which to choose that this should present few difficulties. Most people like light cold desserts, or when fruit such as raspberries or strawberries are in season, nothing could be nicer than to serve these with cream or ice cream.

Cheeses

Try to have an interesting selection of cheese. Cheddar and Cheshire are always a wise choice. Have a really strong flavoured cheese such as Gorgonzola or Stilton; an interesting cheese which may be unknown to some people (this is always a good topic of conversation) – Samsoe, Tome au Raisin, Emmenthal (an interesting alternative to the better known Gruyère); smoked cheeses; and a soft cheese that has a very distinctive flavour such as Brie, Camembert or Demi-sel.
Arrange the cheese on a large dish or board; garnish with lettuce, serve with plenty of butter, an interesting selection of cheese biscuits and crispy French bread or rolls, and any salad in season – celery, chicory and radishes are particularly good.

Fruit as a dessert

Many people will enjoy fruit at the end of the meal, and a bowl of beautiful fruit is an attractive decoration in your dining-room. Serve this with small knives so that peeling peaches or pears is easily done, and little bowls of water should be given to each person so they can dip their fingers in this. Real finger bowls are very difficult to obtain, so use soup bowls or cups, and to make them look more interesting, float a tiny flower head in the cold water.

Coffee

Good coffee sets the seal on any meal. Have this all laid out beforehand. Many people will prefer cream or top of the milk in coffee instead of hot milk. Others will prefer to have small cups of black coffee, so take care, on their behalf, that the coffee, while being sufficiently strong to be good, is not over strong.

To serve with drinks

Arrange the following on little dishes so people can help themselves.

Salted nuts

Shell the nuts, heat in butter or olive oil until a faint golden colour, and then toss in salt. Store in air-tight jars or tins.
Almonds should be blanched and dried before salting.

Devilled almonds

Mix a good pinch of curry powder, cayenne pepper, celery salt with the ordinary salt (according to personal taste) – then proceed as above.

Spiced nuts

Add mixed spice, powdered cinnamon, nutmeg and/or ginger to the salt. Adjust this according to personal taste, and proceed as above.

9

Stuffed celery

Fill small pieces of crisp celery with
(a) **Danish Blue** cheese blended with a little seasoned cream or mayonnaise;
(b) **cream cheese** blended with chopped smoked salmon;
(c) **Demi-sel cheese,** blended with a little mayonnaise and finely chopped ham.

Cheese biscuit pastry

This is needed for some of the recipes in this book, but is also a very good basis for tiny biscuits or cheese straws.

cooking time: as recipe or see below

you will need for 24–36 biscuits:

4 oz. flour, preferably plain	little dry mustard
salt	2 oz. butter
cayenne pepper	2 oz. grated cheese
	1 egg yolk

1 Sieve the flour and seasonings together, rub in the butter.
2 Add the cheese and bind with egg yolk, if necessary add a little water as well.
3 Roll out firmly and use for savoury flan or tartlet cases or to make economical cheese biscuits or straws.
4 Bake as individual recipe.
5 Handle carefully when hot since it is very light.

Cheese straws

Make cheese pastry (as before) or for richer pastry use 2½ oz. butter. Roll out the dough and cut into thin fingers. Use a little of the pastry to make rings so that the cheese straws can be threaded through these. Brush with egg white or yolk to glaze. Bake for about 7 minutes in a hot oven (425–450°F.–Gas Mark 6–7).

Cheese and Marmite whirls

Roll out the cheese pastry, above, into a large oblong. Spread with Marmite, roll like a Swiss roll, cut into thin slices and bake for 10–12 minutes, temperatures as cheese straws.

To vary

With chutney – use a fairly smooth chutney instead of Marmite.

Cheese canapés

Cut the dough into tiny rounds or fancy shapes. Bake as for cheese straws, allow to cool, then top with a tiny portion of smoked salmon or pâté.

Ham, apple and blue cheese salad

no cooking

you will need for about 36 cubes:

½-inch thick slice ham	lettuce
6 oz. Danish Blue cheese	chopped green pepper
	parsley
3 red eating apples	French dressing, see
juice 1 lemon	page 28

1 Cut ham into ½-inch thick squares.
2 Roll cheese into small balls.
3 Dice apples leaving peel on and dip into lemon juice to keep their colour.
4 Line a dish with lettuce and make piles of cheese, ham and apple.
5 Sprinkle with chopped green pepper and garnish dish with parsley.
6 Serve with French dressing for main dish but delicious with cocktails. Put on cocktail sticks to serve.

Variation

Melon and ham salad – follow the basic recipe above, but use balls or squares of melon instead of apple. A Dutch cheese can be used in place of blue cheese.

Anchovy fingers

cooking time: 20–25 minutes

you will need for 32 fingers:

6 oz. plain flour	2 oz. butter
pinch salt	2 level teaspoons
4 oz. Cheddar cheese	anchovy essence

1 Sieve flour and salt into a basin. Grate cheese.

2 Rub in butter and mix in cheese.

3 Stir in anchovy essence and knead into a smooth dough, adding water if necessary.

4 Roll out to an oblong 9×5-inches and cut into fingers 2½×½-inch.

5 Place on baking sheets and bake in a very moderate oven (350°F.–Gas Mark 3) for 20–25 minutes until crisp and golden brown.

Variations

Tomato and Parmesan – use 2 teaspoons tomato ketchup in place of essence and 2 oz. grated Parmesan cheese, 2 oz. grated Cheddar cheese instead of all Cheddar cheese.

Marmite – use Marmite instead of anchovy essence. Since this is is rather sticky, you may find it better to work into the butter, cream this with the cheese, then add the flour.

Menus

Chicken liver en surprise

cooking time: 15–20 minutes

you will need for 4 servings:

4 chicken livers, fresh or frozen	2 tablespoons cream
1 oz. butter	4 oz. creamed potato
little seasoning	parsley
3 tablespoons grated cheese	paprika pepper

1 Arrange the washed and dried livers in an ovenproof serving dish.

2 Top with butter and seasoning.

3 Heat for approximately 5 minutes in a hot oven (425–450°F.–Gas Mark 6–7).

4 Top with two tablespoons of the cheese, cream and a wafer-thin coating of potato and the rest of the cheese.

5 Cook for a further 10–15 minutes.

6 Serve garnished with chopped parsley and paprika pepper.

Sole Véronique

cooking time: 45 minutes

you will need for 4 servings:

2 medium-sized soles	1 can evaporated milk or ¼ pint cream or milk
2–3 peppercorns	
few parsley stalks	
½ pint water	1 oz. butter
seasoning	1 oz. flour
3 tablespoons white wine	4 oz. green grapes

1 Have the soles skinned and filleted.

2 Put the heads and bones into a saucepan with the peppercorns and parsley stalks and ½ pint water.

3 Simmer for 30 minutes, then strain off the stock and retain.

4 Season the fillets and roll them skin side in, or skin if wished.

5 Place upright on a buttered deep plate or dish.

6 Add stock and wine, cover and poach in a moderate oven (375°F.–Gas Mark 4) or over a pan of water until cooked.

7 Strain off liquor and make up to just over ½ pint with evaporated milk.

8 Keep fish hot.

9 Make a white sauce with butter, flour, and milk liquid.

10 Heat the grapes in a little wine or bring to the boil, then skin and stone.

11 Coat the fish evenly with the sauce and garnish with the grapes.

Variations

Sole in white wine – omit the grapes, and use all wine in place of wine and cream. Garnish with finely chopped parsley. A little more flavour can be added by putting a small onion or shallot in at stage 6.

Sole Normandy – omit the grapes in Sole Véronique and add prepared or canned mussels and prawns to the sauce.

French apple flan with redcurrant glaze

cooking time: 30–40 minutes

you will need for 4–6 servings:

6 oz. fleur pastry, see page 22
2 lb. cooking apples
4 oz. castor sugar
4 tablespoons redcurrant jelly

1 Line an 8-inch flan case with the pastry, decorate the edge and bake 'blind' in a hot oven (450°F.–Gas Mark 7) for 10 minutes to set the pastry but do not brown.
2 Remove and cool.
3 Meanwhile peel, core and slice apples thinly.
4 Pack into pastry case, sprinkling each layer with sugar.
5 For the top layer, arrange the apple slices round the case, overlapping each other in circles.
6 Sprinkle with rest of sugar and bake in a moderate oven (375°F.–Gas Mark 4) for 20–30 minutes, or until pastry is cooked and apples tender.
7 Meanwhile, melt redcurrant jelly slowly in a pan, but do not allow it to boil.
8 If necessary, strain it.
9 Paint the glaze on to the apples taking care to fill in all cracks.
10 Leave to cool and serve.

Variation
Apricot glazed apple flan – use sieved apricot jam in place of redcurrant jelly, together with 2 or 3 drops of almond essence.

Smoked salmon or trout

Arrange one or two slices smoked salmon on plates with a good wedge of lemon. Garnish with tiny lettuce leaves. Serve with cayenne or paprika pepper and thin brown bread and butter.
Smoked trout is served with horseradish cream. Allow one per person.

Steak with pineapple and cherries

cooking time: 20 minutes

you will need for 4 servings:

4 oz. butter
1 medium-sized can pineapple pieces
¼ pint port wine
1 small can red cherries
pinch salt
dash cayenne pepper
4 slices toast
4 fillets steak, 1-inch thick

1 Melt 1 oz. butter in a saucepan.
2 Add pineapple pieces, ¼ pint pineapple syrup, port wine and cherries, and simmer for 20 minutes, adding seasonings.
3 Melt half the remaining butter in frying pan and place the toast in it.
4 Fry for 30 seconds on each side, remove and keep hot.
5 Melt the remaining butter in the same frying pan and place the fillets in it.
6 Fry for 3–4 minutes on each side.
7 Place the toast on a large dish, put a fillet on top of each slice and pour sauce on top.

Queen Mab's pudding

cooking time: 5–10 minutes

you will need for 4 servings:

Egg custard made with:
3 eggs
1 pint milk
1–2 oz. sugar
1½ level dessertspoons powdered gelatine
4 tablespoons hot water
2 oz. chopped glacé cherries
2 oz. chopped crystallised peel
¼ pint lightly whipped cream

To decorate:
little whipped thick cream
glacé cherries

1 Make a 1 pint custard thick enough to coat spoon, see page 29.
2 Dissolve the gelatine in the hot water.
3 Stir into hot custard, add chopped glacé cherries, peel and whipped cream.
4 Put into mould.
5 When set turn out of mould and decorate with cream and cherries.

Ginger orange pudding

Make the 1 pint custard as recipe before. Dissolve the gelatine in 4 tablespoons hot orange juice, add to the custard with 2–3 oz. chopped crystallised orange peel. When cool, but not set, fold in the whipped cream. Put into rinsed mould, turn out and decorate with slices of fresh orange and pieces of crystallised ginger.

Avocado pears

no cooking

you will need for 4 servings:

2 avocado pears
French dressing,
  see page 28

little lemon juice

1 Halve the avocado pears just before serving.
2 Remove stones, and fill with French dressing.
3 If halving the pears some little time before the meal, they must be sprinkled with a little lemon juice to prevent discoloration.
4 Avocado pears are an acquired taste, so ascertain everyone will like these, or serve an alternative.

Crusted savoury steaks

cooking time: 20–25 minutes

you will need for 4 servings:

For marinade:

1 clove garlic, crushed, optional
1 grated onion
2 tablespoons oil
seasoning
few peppercorns
1 teaspoon dried herbs
2 tablespoons vinegar or lemon juice

4 tablespoons red wine

4 portions fillet, porterhouse, or rump steak
2 tablespoons butter } for
2 tablespoons oil } frying

For cheese pastry:

8 oz. plain flour
1 level teaspoon baking powder
½ level teaspoon salt
4 oz. butter or margarine

2 oz. grated cheese
water

egg to glaze
oil for frying

For piquant sauce:

4 oz. grated cabbage
1 dessertspoon finely chopped parsley

approx. ¼ pint whipped cream or mayonnaise

1 level dessertspoon grated onion
1 level dessertspoon sugar
1 teaspoon lemon juice

1 dessertspoon vinegar
2 gherkins, finely chopped

1 Mix all ingredients for the marinade.
2 Trim away excess fat and any bone from the steaks and marinate for at least 2 hours.
3 Remove, drain and fry quickly in hot butter and oil until seared on both sides.
4 Remove and drain.
5 Prepare pastry, see page 10, roll thinly and cut into eight rounds.
6 Place each steak on a pastry round, glaze edges with beaten egg and cover with another round, press edges well together to seal.
7 Fry covered steaks in hot oil until golden brown on both sides.
8 Serve piping hot with piquant sauce, made by combining all the ingredients and chilling.
9 To keep hot, put on kitchen paper in low oven for short time.

Variations

Steaks en croûte – follow the recipe above to stage 6. Bake in a hot oven for 20 minutes, then lower the heat to moderate for a further 10 minutes. Serve with piquant or tomato sauce. If preferred use ordinary short crust pastry instead of cheese pastry.

Ham en croûte – choose thick slices of ham, fry as stage 3 then wrap in cheese or short crust pastry and bake for 20 minutes in a hot oven, then 10 minutes in a moderate oven. Serve with piquant or tomato sauce.

Peach mousse

cooking time: few minutes

you will need for 4 servings:

6 fresh ripe peaches
½ packet lemon jelly

1 small can evaporated milk OR ¼ pint thick cream

To decorate:

little thick cream OR evaporated milk

angelica

1 Skin and sieve four of the peaches, halve, stone and slice the remaining two.
2 Make up the jelly to ¼ pint with boiling water, chill until thick and then whisk well.

continued

3 Whisk the evaporated milk or cream until firm enough to hold shape.
4 Whip the two mixtures together and fold in the sieved peaches.
5 Leave to set in four glasses.
6 Arrange the peach slices on top of the mixture and decorate with whipped evaporated milk or cream, and angelica.

Variation

Pineapple and lemon mousse – use a medium can pineapple rings instead of the ripe peaches and also 1 large or 2 medium lemons, rest of ingredients as Peach Mousse.

Drain and chop about 4 pineapple rings and cut the rest of the pineapple rings into neat pieces.

Make up the jelly with enough boiling syrup from the pineapple rings and lemon juice to give ¼ pint, chill and whisk well. As stage 3 above. As stage 4 above, but add the chopped pineapple. As stage 5 above. Decorate with the pineapple pieces, evaporated milk or cream, and angelica.

Grilled salmon

cooking time: see recipe

you will need for 6 servings:

approximately 1½ lb. fresh salmon	butter

To serve and garnish:

parsley	Hollandaise sauce, see page 28
lemon	

1 The salmon can either be cooked in one of the ways suggested on page 44, and served hot.
2 Or it can be cut into six portions, brushed with melted butter, and cooked under the grill for approximately 10 minutes.
3 Serve garnished with parsley, lemon, and with Hollandaise sauce.

Variations

Fried salmon – coat the salmon in seasoned flour, then in egg and crumbs, and either deep fry for a few minutes, or fry in shallow fat. Serve with Hollandaise or tartare sauce, see pages 28 and 44.

Grilled salmon with soured cream sauce – grill the salmon as before, stage 2, then spread with soured cream, flavoured with chopped fresh parsley, finely chopped capers and a little paprika. Heat for 1–2 minutes only, under the grill, then serve with lemon.

Roast lamb

Roast lamb is at its best in the spring. Choose shoulder, leg, loin, or even best end of neck of lamb (there is not a lot of meat on this joint so be fairly generous).

cooking time: see below

you will need for 6 servings:

1 small leg or shoulder OR ½ large leg or shoulder	OR 3½–4½ lb. loin or best end of neck

1 Roast the lamb in the usual way, allowing 20–25 minutes per lb. and 20–25 minutes over, in a hot oven (425–450°F.–Gas Mark 6–7).
2 Serve with mint sauce, see below, and thin gravy, see page 16.
3 Vegetables to serve at this time of year are the first imported or home grown new potatoes and young broad beans or peas.

Mint sauce

Chop mint finely, add sugar to taste, a little vinegar, and if liked a little hot water.

Cucumber sauce

Peel a medium sized cucumber, cut into small neat strips. Toss in 2 oz. butter or margarine, then simmer in about ½ pint white stock until tender. Sieve or put into the liquidiser goblet until a smooth purée, then blend with ¼ pint thick cream and seasoning. This is delicious with hot or cold lamb or with cooked fish.

Gooseberry charlotte pie

cooking time: about 1 hour

you will need for 4 servings:

1½ lb. gooseberries	2 oz. raisins
4 oz. sugar	2 oz. currants
1 level teaspoon cinnamon	grated rind ½ lemon

For pastry :*

8 oz. flour
6 oz. butter
1 oz. sugar
1 egg yolk
juice of ½ small lemon
*or use 8–10 oz. short crust pastry.

1 tablespoon cold
  water
little granulated sugar
  and milk to glaze

1 Top and tail gooseberries and mix with the other ingredients.
2 To make pastry, rub butter into sifted flour until mixture resembles fine breadcrumbs.
3 Stir in sugar and mix in egg yolk, lemon juice and water.
4 Wrap and chill for 1 hour.
5 Divide pastry into two parts, one part being twice as big as the other.
6 Roll out larger piece to line an 8-inch pie plate.
7 Fill with fruit mixture and top with rest of pastry rolled out to fit.
8 Score top in diamond pattern, brush lightly with milk and sprinkle with tablespoon granulated sugar.
9 Bake in centre of a hot oven (425–450°F.–Gas Mark 6–7) for 20 minutes, then lower heat to 375°F.–Gas Mark 4 for another 30–40 minutes.
10 Delicious hot or cold with whipped cream or ice cream.

Variation

Apple charlotte pie – use 1½ lb. apples instead of gooseberries. Peel and slice thinly and mix with other ingredients. Use raisins and sultanas instead of raisins and currants if wished.

Cheese-topped steaks

cooking time: according to taste

you will need for 4 servings:

1½ oz. butter
4 rump or fillet steaks
seasoning
4 oz. cottage cheese

1 level teaspoon
  paprika
2 teaspoons chopped
  parsley

1 Melt a little of the butter and brush the steaks on both sides.
2 Season and grill the steaks according to personal taste.
3 Mash the remaining butter until soft.
4 Gradually add this to the cottage cheese and stir in the paprika and parsley thoroughly.

5 Immediately before serving pile a spoonful of the garnish on top of each steak.
6 This dish is better if you do not have an hors-d'oeuvre, as it needs to be served immediately.

Peach dumplings and lemon almond sauce

cooking time: 25–30 minutes

you will need for 4 servings:

12 oz. short crust
  pastry, see page 72

4 teaspoons semolina
  or breadcrumbs
egg or milk to glaze

For filling:
4 large ripe peaches
1½ oz. sugar

2 teaspoons cinnamon

For sauce:
2 teaspoons arrowroot
½ pint cold water
4 oz. sugar

juice of 1 lemon
½ teaspoon almond
  essence

1 Roll pastry out thinly into four squares about 6½ × 7-inches.
2 Sprinkle each square with a teaspoon of the semolina or breadcrumbs.
3 Skin the peaches by plunging them into hot water for a minute, then peeling.
4 Leave them whole and place one in the middle of each pastry square.
5 Mix the cinnamon and sugar together and sprinkle a little over each peach.
6 Moisten the edges of the pastry with water and pull up the four corners to meet and cover the peach.
7 Press the joins well together to seal, and place, joined side down on greased baking sheet.
8 Brush with beaten egg or milk, decorate with pastry leaves made from trimmings and bake in the centre of a hot oven (425–450°F.–Gas Mark 6–7) for 25–30 minutes.
9 To make the sauce, mix the arrowroot with a little of the water.
10 Cook the sugar and the rest of the water gently, until sugar dissolves.
11 Pour a little of the hot syrup on to the arrowroot mixture, stir until smooth and return all to pan.
12 Continue stirring and cooking until boiling and clear.
13 Remove from heat and stir in the lemon juice and almond essence.

Devils on horseback

cooking time: few minutes

you will need for 4 servings:

8 large juicy prunes, cooked	butter
	paprika
4 long rashers bacon	little pâté, optional
8 toast fingers	

1 Stone the prunes, cut each rasher of bacon into half and wrap round the prunes, securing with cocktail sticks.
2 Cook under grill until bacon is crisp and brown.
3 Serve on buttered toast, dusted with paprika.
4 If wished, a little liver pâté, see below, can be inserted into the centre of the prunes.

Variation

Angels on horseback – follow the recipe above, but use either small oysters or large prepared mussels instead of prunes.

Pâté de foie gras

cooking time: 25 minutes

you will need for 4 servings:

1 large or 2 smaller goose livers	2 tablespoons cream
	1 tablespoon brandy
small portion of a clove of garlic	butter
	seasoning

1 Mince the liver and mix with the other ingredients.
2 Put into a small well-buttered dish, top with buttered paper.
3 Stand in a dish of cold water to keep the pâté from drying and cook for approximately 25 minutes in a very moderate oven (300–350°F.–Gas Mark 2–3). Remove from oven.
4 When the pâté is cold, cover with a layer of melted butter.
5 To serve, cut in slices, arrange on plates with garnish of lettuce, lemon, fans of gherkin, and serve with hot toast and butter.

Variations

Chicken pâté – use approximately 8–12 oz. frozen or fresh chicken livers (duck's could also be used).

Liver pâté – use ordinary liver in place of goose liver.

Piquant flavoured pâté – omit the cream, moisten with a little stock, add 1 teaspoon finely chopped onion, gherkin, plenty of seasoning and 2 oz. finely minced bacon, cover with bacon rashers.

Creamed pâté – use $\frac{1}{4}$ pint thick white sauce and 3 tablespoons cream, adding an egg yolk to the minced liver, this will take about 10 minutes longer to set.

Boned stuffed shoulder of lamb

A boned shoulder of lamb enables a good amount of stuffing to be put in and at the same time makes a difficult joint simple to carve.

cooking time: see method

you will need for 6–10 servings:

1 boned shoulder of lamb	OR
	raisin and apple stuffing, see page 17
sage and onion stuffing OR	fat for roasting
veal stuffing, see page 37	

1 Make the stuffing.
2 Press into the cavity of the shoulder in place of the bone and shape well.
3 Tie with string and roast with fat in a hot oven (425–450°F.–Gas Mark 6–7).
4 Allow 20–25 minutes per lb. and 25 minutes over (weigh after stuffing).
5 Serve with thickened gravy, see below.
6 If you wish to roast without stuffing, an onion sauce, see page 17, is an ideal accompaniment to roast lamb.

To make gravy

Thin gravy

1 Pour away practically all the fat from the roasting tin, leaving the residue of meat to give flavour.
2 Add about 1 teaspoon flour and approximately $\frac{1}{2}$ pint stock, or water flavoured with meat or vegetable extract or bouillon cube.
3 Bring to the boil, cook until clear and strain.

Thickened gravy

1 Leave about 1 tablespoon fat in the meat tin.
2 Add approximately 1 oz. flour.
3 Cook, stirring, until browned.
4 Add just over $\frac{1}{2}$ pint stock or water flavoured with meat or vegetable extract or a bouillon cube.
5 Bring to the boil, cook until thick and strain.

Sage and onion stuffing

cooking time: 20 minutes

you will need:

2 large peeled onions
½ pint water
1 oz. suet or butter
good pinch salt and
pepper

2 oz. breadcrumbs
1 teaspoon dried sage
1 egg

1 Put the onions into a saucepan, adding ½ pint water, and simmer steadily for 20 minutes. Strain.
2 Chop the onions finely, then mix with the other ingredients. Add a little onion stock, if wished.

To vary

Whether you make your own stuffing or buy the packet stuffing try:

(a) **Apple** – add a medium peeled grated dessert apple at stage 3.

(b) **Apricots** – add about 2 tablespoons sliced canned apricots (excellent with duck).

(c) **Celery** – add about 4 tablespoons chopped celery and 1 chopped green pepper. This is very good with pork.

Raisin and apple stuffing

no cooking time

you will need:

2 dessert apples
4 oz. fresh white
breadcrumbs
2 oz. chopped raisins
2 oz. chopped
hazelnuts
1 level teaspoon
mustard

1–2 tablespoons
golden syrup
1 dessertspoon oil or
1 oz. margarine
lemon juice
salt, pepper

1 Peel and chop apples.
2 Mix together the apples, breadcrumbs, raisins, hazelnuts and mustard.
3 Heat the syrup and oil and use to moisten the dry ingredients.
4 Add the lemon juice, salt and pepper, and mix.
5 This stuffing is improved with a little 'taste' powder.

Onion sauce

cooking time: 20–30 minutes

you will need:

1 oz. butter
1 large onion
1 oz. flour

¾ pint hot stock
salt, pepper
pinch nutmeg

1 Melt the butter in a thick saucepan.
2 Add 1 large sliced onion.
3 Cook gently until tender and golden brown.
4 Sprinkle in flour and stir well.
5 Cook 2–3 minutes, then gradually add the stock, stirring all the time.
6 Season with salt and pepper and simmer gently for 20–30 minutes, stirring from time to time.
7 Season with a pinch of nutmeg.

Variation

Spanish sauce – use the recipe above, but increase the amount of butter to 2 oz. Fry a sliced onion, 2 sliced skinned tomatoes and 2–3 sliced mushrooms in this, then proceed as the onion sauce.

Apricot and vanilla bavarois

cooking time: 30 minutes

you will need for 6–8 servings:

4 oz. dried apricots
¾ pint water
2 oz. sugar
1 tablespoon lemon
juice

3 level teaspoons
gelatine
2 tablespoons cold
water

For vanilla:

2 level teaspoons
gelatine
4 tablespoons cold
water
2 eggs

1½ oz. sugar
½ pint milk
vanilla essence
½ pint thick cream

1 Wash and soak the apricots in ¾ pint water overnight.
2 Add sugar, lemon juice, and cook over a low heat until apricots are tender. Sieve.
3 Soften gelatine in two tablespoons cold water and dissolve over pan of boiling water.
4 Add dissolved gelatine to apricot purée and pour into an oiled 2-pint mould.
5 Soften the gelatine for the vanilla in the four tablespoons cold water and dissolve over boiling water. Cool.
6 Beat the eggs with the sugar, milk, and vanilla essence, stir over boiling water until the mixture becomes hot. Cool.
7 Add the dissolved gelatine.
8 Fold in the beaten cream.
9 Pour over the set apricot mixture in the mould, and chill. Turn out.

Variation

Chocolate and vanilla bavarois – omit the apricot layer and stages 1–4. Use double the ingredients for the vanilla layer and prepare as stages 5–8. Spoon half the mixture into another basin and carefully fold in 2 oz. chocolate powder. Spoon this chocolate layer into an oiled 2-pint mould, then spoon the vanilla layer on top and allow to set, then turn out.

Prawn cocktails

no cooking

you will need for 4 servings:

lettuce
lemon juice, optional

6–8 oz. shelled prawns

For cocktail sauce:

3–4 tablespoons
  mayonnaise
1 tablespoon tomato
  purée, fresh or from
  tube

OR tomato ketchup
few drops tabasco
  and/or chilli sauce
little extra seasoning

To garnish:
lemon slices

1 Shred the lettuce very finely.
2 Put into glasses with a squeeze of lemon juice, if wished.
3 Toss the prawns in the sauce, which is made by mixing all the ingredients together.
4 Pile on top of the lettuce and garnish with lemon slices.

Variations

Mixed fish cocktails – a more economical cocktail can be made by using a small quantity of shellfish and flaked white fish.

Crab and pineapple cocktails – substitute a medium sized dressed crab or a can of crabmeat for the prawns. Use a small can pineapple pieces. Follow stages 1 and 2 above. Blend the flaked crabmeat with the dressing and most of the well drained pineapple pieces. Pile on top of the lettuce and garnish with the remainder of the pineapple pieces.

Chinese lamb stew

cooking time: 50 minutes

you will need for 4 servings:

8 lamb cutlets
seasoned flour
little oil
1 dessertspoon
  chopped onion
½ can bamboo shoots
3 water chestnuts

2 oz. mushrooms
2–3 stems celery, or
  canned celery
approximately ¾ pint
  stock or water
soy sauce to taste

To garnish:
1 medium-sized
  cucumber
salt

oil
good pinch castor
  sugar

1 Trim cutlets, dust with seasoned flour, and fry lightly on both sides in hot oil with finely chopped onion.
2 Transfer to casserole, add chopped bamboo shoots, water chestnuts and thinly sliced mushrooms, and chopped celery.
3 Barely cover with stock or water, stir in soy sauce.
4 Cover with lid or foil and cook in moderate oven (375°F.–Gas Mark 4) for 40 minutes or until meat is tender.
5 Serve with 'slices of the moon', i.e. slice a cucumber lengthways and place in long dish, trimming away any tough seeds.
6 Sprinkle with about 1 tablespoon salt, leave for 30 minutes.
7 Drain off liquid – dabbing surplus off with clean cloth.
8 Fry in heated oil on both sides, sprinkle with sugar and serve.

Peach lemon soufflés

cooking time: few minutes

you will need for 6 servings:

1 small can sliced
  peaches

½ pint thick lemon
  custard*
1 oz. butter

Soufflé mixture:

1 lemon
2 eggs
5 tablespoons milk
1 heaped tablespoon
  sugar, or to taste

1 level teaspoon
  gelatine
5 teaspoons water
5 dessertspoons
  unwhipped thick
  cream

To decorate:

about 4 tablespoons whipped thick cream	quartered glacé or canned stoned cherries

*Make ½ pint custard and flavour with grated lemon rind and sugar as liked.

1 Drain the peaches and divide equally between six sundae glasses.
2 Make custard and add butter.
3 Pour over fruit in glasses, leave until cold.
4 To make soufflé mixture, grate lemon rind finely, taking care not to include any white pith.
5 Squeeze out the juice.
6 Separate the eggs, boil the milk and sugar and pour over beaten egg yolks, stirring all the time.
7 Stand basin over hot water and stir over a low heat until thick, do not allow to boil.
8 Dissolve gelatine in the water over a low heat.
9 Strain into egg mixture and stir in lemon juice and rind and the unwhipped cream, cool, but do not set.
10 Whisk egg whites very stiffly, lightly fold into egg yolk mixture.
11 Pile lightly into sundae glasses, leave to set.
12 Decorate with rosettes of whipped cream in centre of each sweet.
13 Arrange cherries round to represent flower petals.

Crab and celery canapés

cooking time: few minutes for frying croûtons

you will need for 4 servings:

1 small crab or medium-sized can crabmeat	cream dressing, see page 19, with few drops tabasco sauce added
6 tablespoons chopped celery and parsley	fried bread croûtons

For French dressing:

3 tablespoons oil	salt and pepper
1 tablespoon vinegar	few drops tabasco sauce
1 teaspoon French mustard	

1 Mix ingredients for dressing.
2 Marinate the white crabmeat in the dressing for about 1 hour. Drain.

3 Add chopped celery and parsley and mix with the cream dressing to a soft spreading consistency.
4 Serve on fried croûtons, see page 36, garnished with the dark crabmeat.

Variation

With salad – if preferred, serve on a bed of green salad instead of fried bread.

Cream dressing

you will need:

3 tablespoons mayonnaise	good squeeze lemon juice OR little wine vinegar
3 tablespoons lightly whipped cream	seasoning

Mix all the ingredients thoroughly together.

Tipsy pork chops

cooking time: about 25 minutes

you will need for 4 servings:

1 oz. lard	¼ pint red wine
2 cloves garlic, chopped	1 tablespoon chopped parsley
4 loin, or spare rib, pork chops	salt and pepper
	1 lemon

1 Heat the lard in the frying pan and add the garlic.
2 Add the chops and fry both sides for about 8–10 minutes.
3 Add the wine, parsley and seasoning.
4 Cover with a lid and cook for further 15 minutes, when most of the liquid is absorbed.
5 Serve garnished with lemon and serve with creamed potatoes, see page 48.

Variation

Paprika pork chops – use the recipe above, but add 2 teaspoons paprika blended with ¼ pint soured cream or use thick fresh cream instead. Proceed as above to stage 4, retaining an appreciable amount of the wine. When the chops are tender lift on to a hot dish. Blend the paprika flavoured cream with the wine and simmer for 2–3 minutes, then pour over the pork chops and garnish with lemon and serve with creamed potatoes.

Deloraine chiffon surprise

cooking time: few minutes OR 1 hour

you will need for 4 servings:
Ginger nut crust:

6 oz. ginger nut biscuits
1 teaspoon mixed spice
3 oz. butter

2 tablespoons brown sugar
½ teaspoon lemon essence or juice

For filling:

2 egg yolks
½ pint sweetened condensed milk

¾–1 pint cooked unsweetened apple purée

For meringue topping:

2 egg whites
4 oz. castor sugar

2 oz. blanched almonds

1 Crush biscuits by rolling between sheets of greaseproof paper.
2 Place in basin and add spice.
3 Melt butter and add sugar and essence or juice.
4 Pour on to biscuits and mix well.
5 Press mixture into 8-inch pie dish approximately 1½ inches in depth.
6 Chill until set and firm.
7 Beat yolks for filling into milk.
8 Cook over low heat without boiling.
9 Fold in apple purée, cool and spread into pie case.
10 For meringue beat whites until very stiff.
11 Gradually fold in sugar and pipe in a spiral on to top of apple, or pile neatly.
12 Split almonds and sprinkle on meringue and place in hot oven (425–450°F.–Gas Mark 6–7), for 3–4 minutes.
13 Cool and serve immediately.
14 If wishing to make some time before, set meringue for 1 hour in very low oven (275°F.– Gas Mark 1).

Celeriac and tomato prelude

no cooking

you will need for 4 servings:

1 celeriac
mustard
2 tablespoons fresh thick cream

6 tomatoes
French dressing, see page 28
chives

To garnish:

anchovy fillets

mustard and cress

1 Wash and peel the celeriac.
2 Shred it finely and season with dry mustard.
3 Bind with the cream.

4 Skin the tomatoes and dice them.
5 Turn in the oil and vinegar dressing and sprinkle with finely chopped chives.
6 Serve the celeriac and tomatoes in small alternate heaps on a round plate with anchovy fillets in between and garnish with mustard and cress.

Devilled pork spareribs

cooking time: 1¼ hours

you will need for 4 servings:

2 lb. pork spareribs
1 oz. bacon fat

4 tablespoons water
1 grated apple

Marinade:

½ cup red wine*
2 drops hot chilli sauce
3 tablespoons malt vinegar
1 level tablespoon grated onion

½ level teaspoon dry mustard
2 teaspoons Worcestershire sauce
1 level teaspoon salt
¼ level teaspoon paprika

*About 4 good tablespoons

1 Combine all ingredients for the marinade and spread over the ribs.
2 Allow to stand for 2 hours or overnight.
3 Drain the meat and brown on each side in the heated bacon fat.
4 Drain off the fat.
5 Add the marinade and the water to the meat and sprinkle over the grated apple.
6 Cover and simmer over a low heat until the meat is tender, 55–60 minutes.
7 Serve with vegetables as liked.

Cling peach pie

cooking time: 25–30 minutes

you will need for 4–6 servings:
For pastry:

6 oz. plain flour
pinch salt
4 oz. butter

1 tablespoon castor sugar
2–3 tablespoons cold water

For filling:

1 large can sliced peaches
2 tablespoons granulated sugar
2 level tablespoons cornflour

pinch salt
½ teaspoon cinnamon
1 tablespoon butter
milk to glaze
Icing sugar

1 Sieve the flour and salt and rub in the butter.
2 Add castor sugar and mix to a firm dough with the water.
3 Knead slightly and allow to stand in a cool place.

4 Drain juice from peaches and make up to ½ pint with water, if necessary.
5 Place the peaches in an 8-inch round pie dish.
6 Blend the sugar, cornflour, salt and cinnamon with the cold juice and stir over heat until boiling.
7 Cook for 2 minutes.
8 Add butter and pour over the peaches.
9 Roll out pastry into a 9-inch round.
10 Make four 4-inch cuts, diagonally, across the centre.
11 Place over the peaches and turn back the points formed by the cuts.
12 Trim and mark the edge of the pie, glaze with little milk and bake in the centre of a hot oven. (425°F–Gas Mark 6) for 25–30 minutes.
13 Serve hot or cold dusted with icing sugar.

Honey peach pie – omit the granulated sugar in the filling and use 3 tablespoons thin honey instead. Continue to stage 8 and add 2 oz. coarsely chopped almonds in addition to the butter. Proceed as recipe above.

Stuffed egg salad

cooking time: 10 minutes to boil eggs

you will need for 6 servings:

6 eggs	little mayonnaise
1 oz. butter	2 chopped gherkins
2 oz. chopped prawns	little chopped parsley

To garnish:

lettuce	slices tomato
lemon slices	

1 Hard boil the eggs, split lengthways.
2 Scoop out the yolk, mash while hot. If allowed to become cold you will need to sieve.
3 Mix with all the other filling ingredients.
4 Pile back into the white cases, arrange on individual plates or large dish with the salad.

Sardine eggs – mix the yolks with mashed sardines, the oil from the can, and garnish with fans of gherkins.

Asparagus eggs – mix the yolks with chopped cooked or canned asparagus, a little mayonnaise or cream and seasoning. Garnish with asparagus tips.

Curried eggs – mix the yolks with a little butter, curry powder and chutney.
Add a small amount of cream, if wished.

Paprika pork casserole

cooking time: 2¾ hours

you will need for 6 servings:

2–2½ lb. hand of pork	little black pepper
2 oz. fat OR 2 table-	½ teaspoon dried sage
spoons oil	½ pint stock or water
2 onions	and stock cube
1½ oz. flour	juice ½ lemon, optional
2–4 teaspoons paprika	1×14 oz. can tomatoes
1 teaspoon salt	

1 Trim pork of excess fat and cut into neat pieces.
2 Melt the fat in a large pan and fry the sliced onions over gentle heat.
3 Mix the flour, paprika and seasoning, coat the meat with this.
4 Add to onions and cook gently for a few moments, turning several times.
5 Transfer to casserole.
6 Add sage, stock, lemon juice, tomatoes and liquid from can.
7 Cook in centre of a very moderate oven (325–350°F.–Gas Mark 3) in a covered casserole for 2½ hours.
8 Serve with creamed, Duchesse, see pages 46 and 48, or new potatoes, green vegetables.

Walnut pie

cooking time: 40–50 minutes

you will need for 6 servings:

8 oz. flan or fleur	pinch salt
pastry, page 22	½ teaspoon vanilla
4 oz. butter	essence
6 oz. brown sugar	8 oz. coarsely chopped
3 eggs	walnuts*
8 oz. golden syrup	

To decorate:

¼ pint whipped thick	few halved walnuts*
cream	

*If pecan nuts obtainable, use these.

1 Roll out pastry and line a fairly deep 9-inch flan case.
2 Cream butter and sugar.
3 Add eggs, one at a time, beating well.
4 Stir in syrup, salt and vanilla essence.
5 Fold in nuts.
6 Pour into a pastry case and bake in the centre of a moderate oven (375°F.–Gas Mark 4) for 40–50 minutes, until filling is just set and brown.
7 When cool, decorate with whipped cream and halved nuts.

Variation

Honey nut pie – follow the recipe before, but use 8 oz. thin honey instead of golden syrup and use 4 oz. coarsely chopped walnuts, 2 oz. blanched chopped almonds and 2 oz. whole hazelnuts.

Flan or fleur pastry

cooking time: as individual recipe

you will need:

5 oz. butter	pinch salt
1 oz. sugar	1–2 egg yolks
8 oz. flour	water

1 Cream butter and sugar together until light.
2 Sieve the flour and salt together, and add to the creamed butter, mixing with a knife.
3 Gradually add enough egg yolks to make a firm rolling consistency, or use 1 egg yolk and a little water. Use as individual recipes.

Greek lemon soup

cooking time: 20 minutes

you will need for 6–8 servings:

2 pints chicken stock	juice 1 lemon
2 oz. fine semolina	salt, pepper
2 eggs	

1 Heat the stock and shower in the fine semolina.
2 Simmer for 20 minutes.
3 Beat the eggs with the lemon juice.
4 Add about four tablespoons of the very hot stock to this, stirring all the time.
5 Remove the soup from the heat, pour in the egg and lemon mixture, season with salt and pepper. Serve at once.
6 Make sure you do not boil the soup again, once the eggs have been added.

Stuffed turkey legs

cooking time: 35 minutes

you will need for 6–8 servings:

4 oz. chopped bacon	1 tablespoon chopped
1 tablespoon chopped	onion
parsley	2 oz. butter
6 oz. breadcrumbs	1 level tablespoon
little milk	flour
seasoning	½ pint water or stock
4 cooked turkey leg	or tomato juice
joints*	

*i.e. the 2 drum sticks, 2 thighs.

1 Mix bacon, parsley, breadcrumbs and little milk to bind together, adding seasoning to taste.
2 Cut down leg joints and remove bones.
3 Press stuffing in side and skewer or tie into position.
4 Fry onion in butter and add flour, stir for several minutes.
5 Add water or stock, bring to the boil and cook until slightly thickened.
6 Add leg bones, seasoning and stuffed legs.
7 Cover pan and simmer for about 30 minutes.
8 To serve remove bones, cut leg joints in slices.

Variations

Stuffed chicken legs – large legs of chicken may be stuffed instead of turkey. There is no need to cook these completely. Cover in buttered foil and cook for about 20–25 minutes in a moderately hot oven. Split, bone, and stuff.

Mushroom stuffed legs – fry 4 oz. chopped mushrooms and 1 chopped onion in 2 oz. butter. Add a little chopped parsley, chives, and 2 tablespoons soft breadcrumbs. Season well. For a chicken you will not need so much stuffing, but for a turkey you may need a little more than this.

Viennese pudding

cooking time: 2½ hours

you will need for 6–8 servings:

3 oz. loaf OR	2 oz. sultanas
granulated sugar	2 oz. chopped glacé
3 tablespoons water	cherries
1 pint milk	2 oz. chopped nuts,
4 oz. bread, without	optional
crusts	1 oz. finely chopped,
1½ oz. castor sugar	crystallised peel
4 egg yolks	2 tablespoons sherry,
2 egg whites	optional

1 Put the loaf or granulated sugar and water into a strong pan, stir until the sugar has dissolved, then boil steadily until dark brown.
2 Cool slightly, then add the milk and heat without boiling until the milk has absorbed the caramel, then pour over the diced bread.
3 Allow to soak for at least 30 minutes.

4 Add all the other ingredients to the caramel mixture, beating the eggs very well before they are put in.

5 Pour into a greased basin and steam gently, without boiling, for approximately 2½ hours.

6 Cool for 3 minutes in the basin so the pudding has a chance to settle, then turn carefully on to a hot dish.

7 Serve with cream or with sherry-flavoured custard or either of the following sauces.

Variation

Orange caramel pudding – use the recipe above, but omit the castor sugar and substitute the rind of 2 fresh oranges and 2–3 tablespoons orange marmalade. Make the caramel as stage 1, but do not allow the sugar and water to become too brown. Add the orange rind and the marmalade, then continue as the recipe.

Sherry sauce

cooking time: few minutes

you will need for 6–8 servings:

1 oz. sugar	3 tablespoons sweet
2–3 egg yolks	sherry
4 tablespoons thin cream or top of milk	

1 Put all the ingredients, except the wine, in a basin over pan of steadily boiling water.

2 Whisk until thickened and fluffy.

3 Add wine, whisk again.

Variation

Marsala sauce – use the recipe as above, but use Marsala in place of cream and sherry.

Foamy sauce

you will need for 4–6 servings:

3 egg yolks	1 tablespoon rum
4 oz. sifted confectioners' sugar	pinch salt
½ teaspoon vanilla essence	¼ pint thick cream

1 Beat egg yolks, sugar, flavourings and salt until very thick.

2 Fold in cream and chill.

3 Stir before using.

4 Delicious also with fruit salad or with Christmas pudding and mincepies.

Cod's roe pâté

no cooking

you will need for 6 servings:

8 oz. smoked cod's roe	squeeze lemon juice
3 tablespoons cream	few drops Tabasco sauce

To serve:
toast or short crust pastry, see page 72

To garnish:

salted almonds lettuce	lemon

1 Blend together cod's roe and cream.

2 Sharpen with a little lemon juice and a few drops of Tabasco sauce.

3 Spread on either fingers of crisp shortcrust pastry and decorate with salted almonds, or serve with hot toast garnished with lettuce and wedges of lemon.

Variation

Kipper pâté – use 8 oz. of well-pounded smoked, cooked or uncooked kippers.

Harlequin rice with veal

cooking time: about 45 minutes

you will need for 6 servings:

2 oz. flour	4 medium-sized
2 teaspoons salt	onions, sliced
¼ teaspoon pepper	1 pint water with
6 veal cutlets	juice ½ lemon
2 oz. oil or fat	1 teaspoon sugar
1 crushed clove garlic, optional	4 oz. rice
2 medium-sized tomatoes	small packet frozen peas

1 Mix the flour with 1 teaspoon salt and the pepper.

2 Dredge the cutlets with the seasoned flour and brown on both sides in the heated oil together with the garlic; remove garlic.

3 Peel tomatoes and chop coarsely.

4 Add to the meat, together with onions, sugar and the liquid, also remainder of the salt.

5 Bring to boil, reduce the heat.

6 Cover with a lid and simmer for about 30 minutes.

7 Remove cutlets, add the rice and peas.

8 Replace cutlets, cover and simmer for about 14–18 minutes, or until rice is tender.

9 Serve with green salad.

Grape gâteau

cooking time: 35–40 minutes

you will need for 6 servings:
For cake:
4 eggs
4½ oz. castor sugar
4 oz. plain flour
1½ oz. margarine, melted
meringues

To decorate:
½ pint thick cream
small bunch green grapes
small bunch black grapes

1 Make the cake, see page 33, omitting baking powder.
2 Bake in a prepared 8–9 inch-round cake tin for 35–40 minutes in a moderate oven (375°F.–Gas Mark 4), cool.
3 Make the meringue with 1 egg white and pipe in small rounds on to a prepared baking tin.
4 Set the meringue, see below.
5 Whisk the cream until stiff.
6 Cut the cake through the centre and sandwich together with about one-third of the cream.
7 Stick the meringues all round the outside with a little cream.
8 Spread remaining cream on top, smooth, then mark with a fork.
9 Decorate with green and black grapes.

Meringues

To each egg white, allow 2 oz. sugar, either 1 oz. castor, 1 oz. icing, or all castor sugar.
Whisk the egg white until very stiff indeed, gradually beat in half the sugar, fold in the rest. Pile or pipe into required shape:
(a) The size of a teaspoon if used for decoration. Baking time: 1–1¼ hours
(b) The size of a large tablespoon to fill with cream or ice cream. Baking time: up to 3 hours
(c) Into a flat base or flan shape to fill. Baking time: 3–4 hours, depending on thickness.
Always put on oiled or buttered tins for easy removal, and bake or 'dry off' at a very low temperature (225–250°F.–Gas Mark 0–¼).
To remove from the tins, dip a palette knife in hot water, shake reasonably dry, insert under meringues.

Parma ham and fresh figs

Serve slices of Parma ham with well-drained canned, or preferably, fresh figs. Pears could be served instead.

Fillets of veal milannaise

cooking time: 15 minutes

you will need for 4 servings:
3 oz. macaroni
3 tablespoons butter or oil
1 large, sliced onion
2 large, skinned tomatoes
4 slices fillet of veal
seasoning

To garnish:
4 slices lemon
1 chopped hardboiled egg
1 teaspoon chopped parsley
small can anchovy fillets

1 Put macaroni to cook in 1 pint salted water.
2 Put half the butter or oil in grill pan, heat, then cook the sliced onion and tomatoes until tender.
3 Meanwhile, put fillets of veal on the grid of grill pan, season and brush with melted butter.
4 Cook on both sides until tender.
5 Drain macaroni, mix with onion and tomato.
6 Season well, and put on dish with veal on top.
7 Garnish with sliced lemon, chopped egg and parsley and anchovy fillets.

Chocolate rum mousse

cooking time: few minutes

you will need for 6 servings:
1½ oz. chocolate powder
½ oz. powder gelatine
¼ pint water
6 oz. marshmallows
3 eggs
2 oz. castor sugar
¼ pint thick cream or evaporated milk
1 tablespoon rum

To decorate:
little whipped thick cream
halved walnuts

1 Put chocolate powder, gelatine, water and 2 oz. marshmallows into a pan and heat VERY SLOWLY until marshmallows and gelatine just dissolve, or stand in basin over hot water.
2 Cool until lukewarm.
3 Beat egg yolks and sugar until very thick then lightly stir into chocolate mixture, together with whipped cream or evaporated milk, rum and remaining marshmallows, snipped into small pieces with wet scissors.
4 Lastly fold in stiffly whisked egg whites.

5 Turn mixture into a 6-inch soufflé dish (1½ pint capacity)*.
6 Chill until set.
7 Remove paper collar, then decorate with whipped cream, piled in the centre, surrounded by walnuts.
*See below for preparing soufflé dishes.

Mocha mousse – follow the recipe above, but use ¼ pint strong coffee instead of water and substitute the liqueur Tia Maria for the rum.

To prepare a soufflé dish

Tie a wide band of greaseproof paper of double or treble thickness around the top of a soufflé dish. Butter lightly the part that stands above the dish. Pin or tie very securely to form a good support to the soufflé or mousse mixture.

Cheese soufflé tarts

cooking time: 15 minutes

you will need for 12 tarts:
short crust pastry, see page 72 made with:
6 oz. plain flour	seasoning
3 oz. fat	water to mix

For filling:
3 eggs	2 oz. grated Parmesan
seasoning	cheese
	pinch mixed herbs

1 Line twelve fairly deep patty tins with the pastry, which must be rolled out very thinly.
2 Beat the eggs with seasoning, add the grated cheese and herbs.
3 Put into the pastry cases and bake for 15 minutes towards the top of a hot oven (425–450°F.–Gas Mark 6–7).

Mushroom soufflé tarts – make the pastry as above. For the filling, slice 2 oz. mushrooms very thinly, toss in ½ oz. butter, add to 3 beaten eggs, seasoning and 1 oz. grated Parmesan cheese. Bake as the cheese soufflé tarts.

Scampi Egyptienne

cooking time: 13 minutes

you will need for 4 servings:
2 small aubergines (egg plants)	lemon juice
seasoning	3 oz. butter
	12 large scampi

To garnish:
1 teaspoon chopped parsley

1 Split the aubergines lengthwise, score the peel, season, add a squeeze lemon juice.
2 Fry steadily for 10 minutes in butter.
3 Put on to a serving dish.
4 Cook the scampi for about 3 minutes in the remaining butter.
5 Pile on top of the aubergines, garnish with chopped parsley and serve at once.

Variations
Fried scampi – coat the scampi with egg and crumbs, fry in hot butter or deep fat for a few minutes only. Serve with lemon and tartare sauce, see page 44.
Scampi meunière – do not coat the fish. Fry in hot butter for about 3 minutes. Lift on to serving dish. Add a little chopped parsley and a squeeze of lemon juice to the remaining butter, pour over the prawns.
Scampi Indienne – mix a little curry powder with the egg and crumbs for coating and fry as above. Serve with lemon or on a bed of boiled rice.
Scampi Provençale – fry a crushed clove of garlic and a very finely chopped onion in oil, together with two chopped skinned, and de-seeded tomatoes. Add the scampi and heat for a few minutes.

Royal veal

cooking time: 10–15 minutes

you will need for 4 servings:
4 veal fillets	1 wineglass dry sherry
2 oz. butter	approx. ¼ pint cream
4 oz. button mushrooms	seasoning

To garnish:
chopped parsley

1 Gently fry veal in the butter until golden and set aside to keep hot.
2 Cook the mushrooms in the butter and arrange over veal.
3 Pour sherry into the pan, cook quickly for 5 minutes, remove from heat, and add cream and seasoning.
4 Pour over veal and sprinkle with parsley.

Variations
Veal Cordon Bleu – put slices of ham and Gruyère cheese on to the fillets of veal, fold to

make a sandwich. Either coat in egg and crumbs or just in seasoned flour and fry steadily in hot butter.

Escalopes of veal – coat the fillets of veal in egg and crumbs, cook in hot butter or butter and oil mixed until crisp, brown and tender, for approximately 10 minutes. Garnish with rings of lemon, chopped hardboiled egg, parsley and capers, or with anchovy fillets.

Veal with pâté – spread the slices of veal with bought or home-made pâté. Fold into a sandwich, coat in egg and crumbs, and fry in hot butter until crisp, brown and tender.

Potato croquettes

cooking time: few minutes

you will need for 4 servings:
1 lb. mashed potatoes
flour
seasoning
1 egg
fine browned
breadcrumbs
little fat for frying

1 The mashed potatoes should be firm enough to form into finger or croquette shapes, if necessary work in a little flour.
2 Coat the shapes with seasoned flour, brush with beaten egg, roll in crumbs.
3 Fry until crisp and brown.
4 Drain very thoroughly on kitchen or tissue paper.

Variations
Potato cheese croquettes – add approximately 2 oz. grated cheese to the creamed potatoes. A very little finely grated cheese can be added to the crumbs for coating. Particularly good with cold chicken or veal.
Savoury potato croquettes – add chopped parsley and a very small amount of grated onion or chopped chives.
Creamed potato croquettes – beat a little cream into the mashed potatoes. Form into croquettes, coat twice since mixture is very soft.

Apple snowballs

cooking time: 1 hour 5 minutes

you will need for 4 servings:
4 cooking apples
little jam
3 egg whites
4–5 oz. castor sugar
4 glacé cherries
8 leaves of angelica
1 Core the apples, slit round the skins for easy removal.

2 Bake for approximately 1 hour in the centre of a moderately hot oven (375–400°F.–Gas Mark 4–5).
3 Lift off the skins.
4 Fill the centre of the apples with a little jam.
5 Whisk the egg whites until very stiff.
6 Gradually fold in the sugar.
7 Spread over the apples completely covering them.
8 Decorate with cherries and angelica and bake the meringue in a very hot oven for about 5 minutes (475–500°F.–Gas Mark 8–9). Serve hot.

Globe artichokes

cooking time: 20–25 minutes

you will need for 4 servings:
4 globe artichokes
seasoning
melted butter
OR
Hollandaise sauce,
see page 28

1 Cut the base of the stem from the artichokes, wash well.
2 Put into boiling salted water, simmer steadily for approximately 20–25 minutes.
3 Serve hot with butter or Hollandaise sauce.
4 To eat the artichokes, peel the outer leaves away, biting the fleshy base.
5 Always put a small knife and fork because the centre of the artichoke needs to be eaten with these.
6 Have finger bowls on the table.

Variation
Cold artichokes with vinaigrette dressing – cook artichokes, allow to become quite cold. Serve with vinaigrette dressing, see page 28, to which has been added finely chopped parsley.

Veal blanquette with prunes

cooking time: about 2¼ hours

you will need for 4–5 servings:
1¼ lb. stewing veal
3 rashers streaky
  bacon
3 carrots
8 oz. button onions or
  shallots
4 oz. prunes
¼ pint white wine
½ pint water or stock
seasoning
little milk
2 oz. butter
2 oz. flour
1 canned red pepper
OR ½ fresh pepper

1 Cut veal and bacon into neat pieces, slice carrots.
2 Blanch the bacon and veal in boiling water, throw away water, and replace meat in pan.
3 Add the onions, prunes and carrots and pour on the white wine and stock.
4 Cover and bring to the boil.
5 Simmer gently for 2 hours, seasoning to taste.
6 Drain off the liquor and measure, add enough milk to give 1 pint liquid.
7 Make a white sauce with this, using the butter and flour.
8 Stir back into the stew and add the strips of red pepper.* Pour into a hot serving dish.

*If using fresh pepper, cook for a short time in salted water.

Variations

Chicken blanquette – use four joints of chicken or boiling fowl. Young chicken will need 1 hour, boiling fowl 2–2½ hours. The prunes and carrots could be omitted and approximately 4 oz. mushrooms fried separately in butter and added to the sauce.

Veal Portuguese – a savoury brown stew can be made if you omit the prunes and substitute 2–3 sliced skinned tomatoes and 3–4 oz. mushrooms for the prunes at stage 3 and brown stock for the milk at stage 6.

Jellied apricot snow

cooking time: 15 minutes

you will need for 4–6 servings:

1 lb. apricots	peel and juice
2–3 oz. sugar	1 lemon
½ pint water	½ oz. powder gelatine
peel and juice	2 egg whites
1 orange	little extra sugar*

*Fold in after egg whites, if needed.

1 Halve the apricots.
2 Boil the sugar and water to make a syrup, put in halved apricots, fruit peels and simmer gently until just tender.
3 Put aside 4–6 apricot halves, rub the rest through a sieve and add to strained syrup together with orange and lemon juice.
4 Add water if necessary to give 1¼ pints.
5 Soften gelatine in a little cold purée, heat the

rest and stir in gelatine until thoroughly dissolved.
6 Cool, and when mixture begins to stiffen fold in stiffly beaten egg whites.
7 Set in mould or glasses.
8 Decorate with the halved apricots and serve with cream or ice cream.
9 Some kernels of apricots could be cracked and either put in the mixture or used for decoration.

Variations

Jellied greengage snow – use 1 lb. greengages instead of apricots.

Jellied rhubarb snow – use 1 lb. ripe rhubarb instead of apricots but substitute fresh or canned orange juice for the water at stage 2 to give a stronger flavour. As rhubarb is a 'watery' fruit, it is best to use just over ¼ pint liquid at stage 2, rather than the ½ pint necessary to cook the apricots.

Asparagus

cooking time: 15–25 minutes

you will need for 4 servings:

1 bundle fresh asparagus	approximately 3 oz. melted butter
salt	

1 To prepare the asparagus, first cut away the base of the white stem so each stalk is the right height to stand upright in the saucepan.
2 Scrape the remaining white stalk until quite green.
3 Wash carefully in cold water.
4 Tie into a bundle or bundles and put into boiling salted water. Cook steadily for 15–25 minutes, depending on thickness of stems.
5 Do not cook too quickly otherwise asparagus falls over and is damaged.
6 Drain well and serve on a hot dish with melted butter.

To serve asparagus

Put a dessertspoon under the plate, tipping it towards the eater; the butter then stays in one place. The asparagus is dipped in hot butter and salt for eating.
As it is eaten with the fingers, have finger bowls or soup cups filled with water and topped with floating flower heads.

Variations

With vinaigrette dressing – cook asparagus as before, and serve cold with vinaigrette dressing, see below, instead of butter.

With Hollandaise sauce – serve hot or cold with Hollandaise sauce, see below.

Vinaigrette (French) dressing

you will need:

2 dessertspoons vinegar (wine vinegar, cider vinegar, or tarragon vinegar)	5 dessertspoons olive oil good pinch salt pepper to taste

Mix all the ingredients thoroughly together.

Hollandaise sauce

cooking time: 10–15 minutes

you will need:

2 egg yolks pinch cayenne pepper salt and pepper	1–2 tablespoons lemon juice or white wine vinegar 2–4 oz. butter

1 Use a double saucepan if possible, if not a basin over a saucepan can be used.
2 Put the egg yolks, seasonings and vinegar into the top of the pan, or basin.
3 Whisk over hot water until sauce begins to thicken.
4 Add butter in very small pieces, whisking in each piece until completely melted before adding the next – DO NOT ALLOW TO BOIL or it will curdle.
5 If too thick add a little cream.

Tartare sauce

Tartare sauce can be based on Hollandaise sauce, instead of on mayonnaise, if wished. Add chopped parsley and capers to the Hollandaise sauce, whether serving hot or cold.

Chicken cacciatore with rice

cooking time: about 1 hour

you will need for 2 large or 4 medium servings:

2 lb. broiler chicken*	1 large can tomatoes
1½ oz. flour	1 small bay leaf
1½ teaspoons salt	2 whole cloves
¼ teaspoon pepper	½ tablespoon chopped parsley
3 tablespoons olive oil	⅛ teaspoon saffron
1 small chopped onion	1 small green pepper
1 small clove garlic	3 tablespoons white wine or sherry

*For a more generous portion, buy 2 chickens or 1 large roasting fowl, which will take 1½ hours to cook.

1 Wash and dry pieces of chicken, after cutting into serving pieces.
2 Mix flour, 1 teaspoon salt, and pepper.
3 Roll chicken in flour mixture.
4 Heat olive oil in a large heavy frying pan.
5 Lightly brown chicken in oil, turning often.
6 Remove from the pan and keep warm.
7 Fry onion and garlic until onion is lightly browned, remove garlic.
8 Add tomatoes, bay leaf, cloves, parsley, remaining ½ teaspoon salt and saffron, stir well.
9 Return chicken to sauce, cover with sliced green pepper.
10 Bring to the boil, reduce heat, cover with a tight lid and simmer for 45–50 minutes.
11 Stir in wine, serve over hot fluffy rice.

Hot fluffy rice

you will need:

6 oz. uncooked rice	½ teaspoon salt
1½ pints broth or bouillon cubes and water	

1 Combine rice, liquid and salt in a saucepan.
2 Bring to boil.
3 Stir, cover and cook over low heat for approximately 20 minutes until rice is tender and liquid absorbed.

Snowden pudding

cooking time: 2 hours

you will need for 4 servings:

2 oz. glacé cherries	2 tablespoons orange or lemon marmalade
4 oz. raisins	
3 oz. breadcrumbs	1 egg
4 oz. shredded suet	little milk
1 oz. flour or rice flour	hot custard sauce, see right
3 oz. sugar	
grated rind 1 lemon	

1 Grease a basin and arrange a thick layer of cherries and raisins at the bottom of it.
2 Mix the rest of the fruit with the crumbs, suet, flour and sugar.
3 Add the lemon rind, marmalade, egg and enough milk to make a sticky consistency.
4 Put over the cherries and raisins, cover.
5 Steam for 2 hours.
6 Serve with a hot custard sauce.

Hot custard sauce

Either make with custard powder as instructed on tin; or use 2–3 eggs or egg yolks to 1 pint milk, sugar and vanilla to flavour, and cook very slowly in the top of a double saucepan until thick enough to coat the back of a wooden spoon. Keep covered with damp paper or a plate to prevent a skin forming, if required cold.

Cream of mushroom soup

cooking time: 20 minutes

you will need for 6–8 servings:
12 oz. mushrooms*	1½ pints water
3 oz. margarine or butter	1¼ pints milk
3 oz. flour	seasoning

*The stems of mushrooms could be used, if liked.

1 Chop mushrooms finely, unless you wish to strain the soup.
2 Melt margarine or butter in saucepan, fry mushrooms for 5 minutes, stirring to prevent discoloration.
3 Stir in the flour and cook for 3 minutes.
4 Remove the pan from the heat and gradually add water and milk.
5 Bring to the boil and cook until soup thickens. Season.

Variation

Cream of asparagus soup – use a large can of asparagus and use any liquid from the can in place of some of the water. If preferred, cook fresh asparagus, and use the liquid in place of water. To serve, rub most of the asparagus through a sieve, but save a few tiny tips for garnish.

Veal roll with prune and apple stuffing

cooking time: 1¾ hours

you will need for 6–8 servings:
4 oz. prunes	1½ lb. minced veal
1 lb. tart apples	1 onion
sugar to taste	2 oz. breadcrumbs
1 lb. flour	lemon juice
½ teaspoon salt	1 egg
5 oz. lard	salt and pepper
scant ½ pint water	1 egg, to glaze

To garnish:
4 small cooking apples   parsley

1 Soak prunes overnight in just enough water to cover them. Simmer until tender.
2 Drain, reserving liquid, remove stones and chop finely.
3 Peel, core and slice apples and cook to a purée in the prune liquid.
4 Add chopped prunes and sweeten to taste with sugar.
5 If the mixture is too thin, bring to the boil and cook for a few minutes, stirring all the time until very firm and thick.
6 To make hot water crust pastry, sieve the flour and salt into a bowl.
7 Place lard and water in a pan and bring to the boil and continue boiling until lard has melted.
8 Pour into flour and mix quickly to a paste.
9 If too dry add extra water. Roll out into a rectangle.
10 Mix finely minced veal, chopped onion, breadcrumbs and lemon juice, bind with egg. Season.
11 Spread veal mixture on to the pastry and cover with prune and apple stuffing, reserving a little.
12 Roll pastry around filling, ensuring that the two ends and the joins are well sealed.
13 Place on a lightly greased baking sheet with the join under the roll.
14 Decorate with trimmings of pastry and brush with beaten egg.
15 Bake in centre of a moderately hot oven (400°F.–Gas Mark 5) for 1 hour or until pastry is golden and cooked.
16 While pastry roll is cooking halve three of the cooking apples and top with the prune and apple purée left.
17 Add the diced fourth apple, bake for approximately 45 minutes.
18 Serve round roll; garnish with parsley.

Raspberry trifle

cooking time: 5 minutes

you will need for 6–8 servings:

1 can raspberries*
4 sponge cakes
little jam or curd
½–1 pint raspberry jelly
½–1 pint custard sauce, see page 29
blanched almonds, optional

ratafias, optional
½ pint thick or 2 cans cream
little sugar

To decorate:

2 oz. blanched almonds
1 oz. chopped pistachio nuts or green coloured almonds, see next column

glacé cherries

*Or use frozen fruit or fresh fruit mashed with sugar.

1 Open the can of raspberries and pour off the syrup.
2 Split sponge cakes and spread evenly with jam or curd.
3 Arrange sponge and some of the raspberries in the bottom of a bowl.
4 Moisten with raspberry syrup and cover with liquid jelly, made with slightly less water than usual, and allow to set.
5 Make the custard sauce and when cool pour over the set jelly; blanched almonds and ratafias can be added to this, if wished.
6 Allow custard to set, putting a plate over the top to prevent a skin forming.
7 Whip the cream until just stiff.
8 Add sugar to taste and spread over the custard, marking with a fork.
9 Split almonds and brown gently under the grill or for about 5 minutes in a moderate oven.
10 Cool and scatter round the edge of the trifle, adding a few pistachio nuts as well.
11 Arrange the remaining raspberries, nuts and glacé cherries in a design in the centre.

Variations

Pear trifle – use canned, sliced pears, flavour milk for custard with almond essence, use lemon jelly.

Mandarin trifle – use canned mandarin oranges, orange curd, and orange jelly.

To colour almonds green

Put a few drops of apple green colouring on a saucer; work dried, chopped blanched almonds into this. Leave in the air to dry for a short time.

Shellfish and avocado salad

no cooking

you will need for 8 hors-d'oeuvre servings:

for 4 main course servings:
4 avocado pears

For salad:

2 cans crabmeat*
3 tablespoons finely chopped celery
½ teaspoon salt
¼ pint mayonnaise

1 tablespoon tomato purée
few drops chilli sauce
1 tablespoon lemon juice

To serve:
lettuce

*Or 1 large crab, or equivalent lobster or shrimps.

1 Mix all salad ingredients, saving 1 teaspoon lemon juice. Chill.
2 Before serving, halve the avocado pears, sprinkle with remaining lemon juice, pile filling high and serve on a bed of lettuce.

Variations

Cheese and avocado salad – dice Blue, Rocquefort, Stilton or Gruyère cheese very finely. Put either into the dressing as given above, or French dressing, see page 28, and serve in the avocado pears. More suitable for light main course.

Prawn and avocado salad – fill the avocado pear halves with prawns in either a French dressing, mayonnaise, or the prawn cocktail sauce, see page 18.

Festive bacon

cooking time: 2 hours 10 minutes

you will need for 8–10 servings:
4½ lb. gammon hock
1 bottle maraschino
  cherries
½ oz. cloves
4 oz. clear honey
salt
cayenne pepper
1 teaspoon dry
  mustard
4 oz. redcurrant jelly

1 Simmer bacon for 1½ hours in a large pan.
2 Remove brown skin and score fat, lattice-fashion, with a sharp knife.
3 Drain cherries, reserving syrup.
4 Cut cherries in half, stud these over surface of bacon with cloves.
5 Put bacon in roasting tin.
6 Add syrup from cherries to honey, seasonings and mustard.
7 Add redcurrant jelly and heat gently until jelly is melted. Brush over bacon.
8 Bake in centre of moderately hot oven (400°F.–Gas Mark 5) for 40 minutes, basting frequently.

Traditional rich trifle

cooking time: 5 minutes

you will need for 8 servings:
4 individual sponge
  cakes
raspberry jam
6 macaroons
12 ratafia biscuits
¼ pint sherry and
  brandy OR sherry
grated rind ½ lemon
1 oz. almonds

For custard:*
½ pint milk
1 egg
1 egg yolk
1 oz. castor sugar

To decorate:
½ pint thick cream
1 oz. castor sugar
1 egg white
cherries
angelica
ratafia biscuits
blanched almonds

*A slightly thicker custard layer can be made, if wished, by using double quantities.

1 Split the sponge cakes in two, spread with jam.
2 Place in bottom of a glass dish with the macaroons and most of the ratafia biscuits.
3 Soak with sherry and brandy, sprinkle on lemon rind and almonds.
4 Leave for about 30 minutes.

5 Make the custard by warming the milk; do not let it boil.
6 Whisk eggs and sugar together, then whisk in warm milk.
7 Return to pan and cook over gentle heat, stirring until custard thickens.
8 Strain, leave to cool slightly, then pour over the soaked sponges.
9 Leave until cold.
10 Whip cream until thick and add sugar.
11 Whisk the egg white until stiff, then fold into the cream.
12 Pile on top of the trifle and decorate with cherries, angelica, a few ratafia biscuits and shredded blanched almonds.

Prawns with Alabama sauce

no cooking

you will need for 4 servings:
For sauce:
½ green pepper
4 sticks celery
1 crushed clove garlic
¼ pint cream dressing
  see page 19
1 tablespoon tomato
  ketchup
1–2 teaspoons chilli
  sauce
1 tablespoon grated
  horseradish
few drops tabasco
  sauce

8–12 oz. prawns
lettuce

1 Chop the pepper and the celery and mix with all the other sauce ingredients.
2 Add prawns and serve on a bed of lettuce.

Variations
Prawns with tomato flavoured mayonnaise – use the recipe for prawn cocktail, see page 18, toss the prawns lightly in the dressing, serve on a bed of green salad and garnish with twists of lemon.

Prawns with cream cheese dressing – use 2 oz. soft cream cheese, and gradually beat the ingredients for the cream dressing into this. Add chopped chives or parsley, and toss the prawns in this. Garnish with lemon and a dusting of red pepper.

Braised duck and cherries

cooking time: 1 hour

you will need for 4 servings:

1 duckling	seasoning
salt	1 lb. Morello cherries
2 oz. butter	4 oz. sugar
1 onion	1 teaspoon lemon
1 carrot	juice
4 tomatoes	little cornflour
1 pint brown stock	little extra sugar
bouquet garni	cherry brandy

To garnish:
watercress

1 Salt the trussed duck inside and out and roast in the butter in a deep tin for 15 minutes.
2 Add the sliced onion, carrot and tomatoes, stock and *bouquet garni*.
3 Season and cover the pan, braise for 45 minutes in a moderate oven (375°F.–Gas Mark 5).
4 Poach the stoned cherries in a syrup made from 1 pint water and the sugar.
5 Remove the cherries and keep hot. Reduce the syrup to half its quantity by boiling hard.
6 Remove the duck from the oven and remove the trussing strings.
7 Pour a little gravy over the duck and keep it hot.
8 Strain ¼ pint gravy into the cherry syrup, add the lemon juice and thicken with a little cornflour, to a coating consistency.
9 Check the seasoning, a little sugar may be required.
10 Remove from the heat and stir a little cherry brandy into the sauce.
11 Pour the sauce over the duck and garnish with the cherries and small sprigs of watercress.

Caramel mousse

cooking time: few minutes

you will need for 4–6 servings:

For caramel:

6 oz. loaf sugar	4 tablespoons water

For soufflé mixture:

3 egg yolks	¼ pint thick cream
3 whole eggs	½ oz. gelatine
3 oz. castor sugar	juice 3 lemons
grated rind 2 lemons	2 egg whites

To decorate:

¼ pint thick cream	pistachio nuts

1 Put the loaf sugar with the water in a pan.
2 Stir until sugar is dissolved and cook slowly until mixture is dark brown caramel.
3 Draw aside, add another three tablespoons cold water, carefully, stir and pour into a bowl to cool.
4 Put the yolks and whole eggs into a bowl with the castor sugar and lemon rind.
5 Whisk until thick over a gentle heat.
6 Remove, cool a little, stir in the caramel, the half-whipped cream, and the gelatine dissolved in the juice of the lemons.
7 Allow to thicken, then fold in the stiffly whisked egg whites.
8 Pour into a lightly oiled mould to set.
9 Turn on to a serving dish and decorate with whipped cream and nuts.

Melon with ginger

no cooking

you will need for 4–5 servings:

1 large melon	**To decorate:**
OR	orange slices
tiny melons, 1 for	OR
each 2 servings	maraschino cherries

To serve:

castor sugar	little sherry, optional
powdered ginger	

1 Cut the large melon into good wedges.
2 The only melons you serve halved are Charontais and Ogen, in which case each person has half the tiny melon. Scoop out the centre seeds, and serve with a spoon and fork.
3 Serve the large melon wedges with a spoon and fork or knife and fork.
4 They look more attractive if the flesh is cut into slices down, loosened all round and left in place on the rind, but pulled out, slightly sideways and alternately to one side and to the other, to give a serrated effect.
5 Decorate with either a twisted orange slice or maraschino cherry.
6 Serve castor sugar, powdered ginger separately.
7 If wished, sprinkle the melon with a little sherry before serving.

Melon and Parma ham – arrange rather small slices of prepared melon with a slice of Parma (smoked) ham. Serve with red pepper.

Veal with paprika

cooking time: about 1 hour

you will need for 4–5 servings:

1¼ lb. veal fillets	salt, pepper
1 oz. flour	1 tablespoon tomato
2 oz. butter	purée
2 onions	½ pint boiling water
1 oz. paprika	1 bay leaf
8 oz. tomatoes	2 tablespoons cream

1 Cut veal into four portions and coat the pieces with flour.
2 Heat 1 oz. butter in pan.
3 Add the floured veal and cook for a few moments until golden all over.
4 Transfer meat and fat to a moderate oven (375°F.–Gas Mark 4) and roast until tender, about 25 minutes, basting from time to time.
5 Meanwhile fry the chopped onions in the remaining butter.
6 When tender, sprinkle in the paprika.
7 Add the chopped tomatoes, salt and pepper and tomato purée.
8 Stir well and allow to cook gently for 5 minutes.
9 Gradually add ½ pint boiling water and the bay leaf.
10 Allow to cook fairly quickly for 20 minutes.
11 Discard the bay leaf.
12 Stir the cream into the sauce and reheat gently before coating the veal with it.

Summer sponge flan

cooking time: as flan

you will need for 4–5 servings:
sponge flan, see right adding 4 drops almond essence to 2 eggs

For filling:

¼ pint thick custard OR	8 oz. black and green grapes, washed and de-pipped
slightly sweetened whipped thick cream	

To decorate:

little whipped thick cream	2 tablespoons strained apricot jam
4–6 oz. strawberries	

1 Make and bake the sponge flan as recipe. Cool.
2 Spread the hollow of the flan with the custard or whipped cream.
3 Arrange the grapes in circles, starting at the rim of the flan.
4 Add whipped cream in the middle of the flan to make a mound and pile strawberries lightly all over the cream.
5 Brush strawberries and grapes generously with the warmed jam.
6 Any remaining strawberries can be put around the base of the flan.

Variations

With wine – sprinkle the sponge flan with Kirsch or Madeira or Sauternes before adding the filling. Half a wineglass should be plenty, as you do not want to soak the cake too much.

Fresh fruit sponge flan – fill the sponge flan with fruit in exactly the same way as a pastry flan. Either coat with glaze, see page 83, or make up ½ pint of a suitably flavoured jelly. Allow this to become half set, then spread over the fruit with a knife dipped in hot water. Decorate with cream.

To make a sponge flan

cooking time: 12–15 minutes

you will need:
For an 8-inch flan:

2 eggs	2 oz. plain flour
2½ oz. sugar	½ level teaspoon
1 oz. butter	baking powder

1 Grease and flour a sponge flan tin.
2 Put eggs and sugar into basin and whisk until thick.
3 Melt butter in pan and allow to cool slightly.
4 Sieve flour and baking powder.
5 Fold flour into the egg mixture with a metal spoon, then fold in the melted butter.
6 Pour into tin; tap the tin gently but firmly as you fill to make sure there are no air bubbles, which could cause 'holes' in mixture.
7 Bake just above centre of moderately hot oven (400°F.–Gas Mark 5) for 12–15 minutes, test to see if cooked by pressing firmly.
8 Wait a few minutes for flan to cool then turn out carefully on to a wire cooling tray.

Orange tomato cocktail

no cooking

you will need for 6 servings:

3–4 sprigs mint	salt
1 pint tomato juice	sugar
¼ pint orange juice	tabasco sauce

1 Bruise the mint.
2 Pour over the tomato juice and the orange juice.
3 Season with salt, sugar and tabasco sauce.
4 Chill thoroughly and allow to infuse at least 1 hour before straining.
5 Strain and serve.

Variation

Tomato juice cocktail – use all tomato juice in place of a mixture of juices, adding seasoning, including celery salt. Add a very little Worcestershire sauce, but allow people to help themselves to additional Worcestershire sauce, if required.

Chicken and mushrooms

cooking time: 3–3½ hours

you will need for 6 servings:

1 large boiling fowl, approx. 5–6 lb.	¼ pint cream or evaporated milk
2 pints water	pepper
black pepper	1 oz. grated Parmesan cheese
1 chopped onion	
little chopped celery	pinch herbs
salt	dash hot chilli sauce
4 oz. butter or margarine	4–6 oz. mushrooms
2 oz. flour	

To garnish:
toasted slivered almonds

1 Quarter the fowl and place in a saucepan with the water, seasoning, onion and celery.
2 Cover and simmer until tender.
3 Remove meat from bone, replace bones in stock, add salt and simmer for 30 minutes to reduce.
4 Strain, cool and skim.
5 Melt 2 oz. butter or margarine, blend in the flour and stir in 1 pint chicken stock and the cream.
6 Heat very slowly, stirring constantly until thickened.
7 Season with salt and pepper, cheese, herbs and chilli sauce.
8 Sauté mushrooms in remaining butter.
9 Place chicken in greased casserole dish and add the mushrooms.
10 Cover with the sauce and bake in a moderate oven (350°F.–Gas Mark 3) for 25 minutes.
11 Sprinkle with almonds and bake a further 10 minutes and serve.

Uncooked cheesecake

no cooking

you will need for 6 servings:

3 eggs	3 tablespoons lemon juice
3 oz. sugar	
grated rind 2 lemons	12 oz. cottage or cream cheese
½ oz. powder gelatine	
3 tablespoons water	¼ pint thick cream or evaporated milk

For lining mould:

1 oz. butter	3–4 oz. fine sweet biscuit crumbs

1 Separate the yolks from the whites of eggs.
2 Beat the yolks, sugar and grated lemon rind until thick and creamy.
3 Dissolve gelatine in the water, and add to the lemon juice.
4 Add this mixture to egg yolks, then add sieved cottage or cream cheese, lightly whipped cream or evaporated milk and the stiffly beaten egg whites.
5 Butter a tin or straight-sided mould and sprinkle lavishly with biscuit crumbs.
6 Put in the cheesecake mixture and allow to set.
7 This is a very fluffy cheesecake.

Fish soufflé

cooking time: 45–50 minutes

you will need for 6–8 hors-d'oeuvre servings:

for 3–4 main course servings:

1 lb. can salmon or tuna fish or cooked white fish	¼ pint thick white sauce, see page 40
4 oz. shrimps	salt
4 eggs	dill seeds

To garnish:
parsley

1 Remove skin and bones from the fish, drain off the liquor, flake the fish.

2 Chop half the shrimps finely, then mix in egg yolks and white sauce.

3 Add salt to taste and dill seeds.

4 Beat egg whites stiffly and fold lightly into fish mixture with most of the remaining shrimps, saving a few for garnish.

5 Turn into a greased 6½-inch soufflé dish and bake for 35–40 minutes in a moderately hot oven (400°F.–Gas Mark 5).

6 Garnish with shrimps and parsley.

Variations

Cheese soufflé – serve at end of meal, after the sweet or in place of the sweet. Use 4 oz. grated cheese, either Cheddar or mixture of Cheddar and Parmesan.

Spinach soufflé – can be served as a first course. Use 8 oz. spinach purée in place of fish.

Parmesan haddock soufflé – use 4 oz. flaked, cooked smoked haddock and 1–2 oz. grated Parmesan cheese.

Economy soufflé – use the yolks of 2 eggs only and the whites of 3 or 4. The remaining egg yolks can be used for Hollandaise sauce, see page 28 or mayonnaise , see page 44.

Sweetbread vol-au-vent

cooking time: 20 minutes

you will need for 4 servings:

8 oz. puff pastry, see page 70	6 oz. raw mushrooms, finely chopped
12 oz. sweetbreads*	1 tablespoon capers
1 egg	¼ pint thick white sauce, see page 40
breadcrumbs	
fat for frying	

To garnish:
slices of mushroom

*Blanch by putting into cold water and bringing to the boil. Throw water away, and simmer sweetbreads for 15 minutes in salted water, cool and skin.

1 Roll out the pastry to ¼-inch thickness.

2 Cut out four medium-sized vol-au-vent cases.

3 Brush the tops with a little egg and bake in hot oven (450–475°F.–Gas Mark 7–8) for 20 minutes, until golden and crisp.

4 Coat the sweetbreads in egg and breadcrumbs and fry until crisp and tender.

5 Meanwhile add the mushroom and capers to the sauce and allow to simmer for 7 minutes.

6 Arrange the pastry cases on individual plates, pile in the sweetbreads and top with the sauce.

7 Garnish with slices of mushroom.

8 Serve with creamed spinach and potatoes.

Variations

Chicken vol-au-vent – diced cooked chicken in place of sweetbreads, adding these to a thick white sauce. Up to ½ pint sauce can be used.

Vegetarian vol-au-vent – make ¼–½ pint of thick creamy cheese sauce, and add approximately 8 oz. diced cooked vegetables with the mushrooms and capers, as basic recipe.

Orange and apple jelly ring

cooking time: 10–15 minutes

you will need for 4–6 servings:

little orange rind	orange colouring
3 oz. sugar	½–¾ oz. gelatine*
¾ pint water	¼ pint orange juice
3 even-sized cooking apples	

To decorate:

angelica	almonds
glacé cherries	fresh orange
whipped thick cream	

*Use only ½ oz. gelatine for firm pears and bananas but ¾ oz. for juicy pears, juicy apples which make more liquid.

1 Cut some orange rind into thin slivers, avoiding the white part.

2 Dissolve sugar in water over a low heat.

3 Put in orange rind and bring to the boil.

4 Peel and core the apples and cut in quarters.

5 Put apples into orange-flavoured syrup with colouring and poach very gently till tender, but not broken.

6 Melt gelatine, in orange juice, over hot water and add to cooling syrup.

7 Strain and leave to get cold.

8 When thick, use a little to coat the bottom of a 7-inch or 8-inch ring mould.

9 Place thin strips of angelica and glacé cherries in this jelly coating to decorate.

10 Add a little more jelly and arrange the apple quarters in this, curved edge down.

11 Gently pour in rest of the jelly.

12 Leave to set and turn out in the usual way.

13 Fill the centre of the fruit ring with lightly whipped cream, see page 7 for lightening cream, and chopped, brown almonds.

14 Decorate with segments of fresh orange.

Variations

Pear jelly ring – in place of segments of orange, use firm dessert pears.

Banana and orange jelly ring – use rather long pieces of banana, adding them at stage 7, when the mixture is cold.

Tomato soup

Serve either ready-prepared tomato soup made more interesting with the addition of a little cream and garnished with chopped parsley and served with croûtons of fried bread, see page 36, or follow the recipe for home-made tomato soup below.

Cream of tomato soup

cooking time: 1 hour 15 minutes

you will need for 8 servings:

2 lb. tomatoes	2 oz. flour
2 onions	1 pint milk
2 carrots	2 oz. butter
2 sticks celery	pinch sugar
little fat bacon	little thin cream,
3 pints stock	optional
salt, pepper	
bouquet garni	

To garnish:

egg whites	croûtons

1 Slice the vegetables.
2 Fry the bacon slowly to extract the fat, then add the vegetables and sauté for about 10 minutes.
3 Add the stock, or water, seasoning, and *bouquet garni*, bring to the boil and simmer gently until tender, about 1 hour.
4 Remove the *bouquet garni*, rub the soup through a fine sieve, and add the flour, blended with the milk and the butter.
5 Return to the pan, bring just to the boil, stirring well, and cook gently for 2–3 minutes.
6 Re-season, add the sugar and serve with your chosen garnish, white of egg finely chopped or cut in shapes, or croûtons.
7 Stir in the cream just before serving.

Croûtons

Slice bread. Cut into ¼-inch dice. Fry in either deep fat or shallow hot butter or oil. Drain and sprinkle on top of soup just before serving or serve separately. Allow 1 tablespoon per person.

Cheese croûtons

cooking time: about 15–20 minutes

you will need:

½ inch thick slices of day old white or brown bread	melted butter grated Cheddar cheese

1 Remove the crust and cut the bread into ½-inch dice.
2 Dip in melted butter, then toss in grated Cheddar cheese to coat thoroughly.
3 Place on a baking sheet and put in a moderately hot oven (400°F.–Gas Mark 5) to crisp and brown, about 15–20 minutes.
4 The croûtons are delicious with many soups.

Roast turkey

A 14 lb. turkey gives ample portions for 10–12 people, or will serve 8 people and leave some over.

Stuff the turkey, the most usual stuffings being: veal, forcemeat, chestnut (see recipes); or some of the less usual recipes also given on page 37.

If using one stuffing only, insert this at the neck end, pulling the skin round firmly to cover this and tying or securing. If serving two stuffings, put one at this end and the other into the body of the bird. Weigh the bird when stuffed. If under 12 lb., allow 15 minutes per lb. and 15 minutes over. If over 12 lb., allow 15 minutes per lb. up to 12 lb., 12 minutes per lb. for each additional lb., plus 12 minutes. Put the bird into the roasting tin, cover with plenty of fat or butter. Either roast uncovered, or roast covered with foil.

There are two ways of using this. Either balloon the foil loosely over the tin to have the effect of a covered roaster; or wrap the bird closely in the foil, and put it into the tin.

In either case, when using foil, allow an additional 15–20 minutes cooking time at least, or use 25°F. or 1 Gas Mark higher, in the oven. The times given assume you are roasting in a hot oven (425–450°F.–Gas Mark 6–7). Modern broad-breasted turkeys tend to need a little longer cooking time than above, so treat this as a minimum.

Rashers of bacon cut and made into bacon rolls; bread sauce and cranberry sauce, see recipes below, are the usual accompaniments to roast turkey.

Cranberry sauce

cooking time: 25 minutes

you will need for 8 small servings:
8–12 oz. cranberries	2–3 oz. sugar
¼ pint water	knob butter

1 Simmer the cranberries in the water.
2 Rub through a sieve, add sugar to taste and a little knob of butter.
3 For an unsieved sauce make a syrup of water and sugar.
4 Drop in the cranberries, cook until a thick mixture, add butter.

Forcemeat stuffing

you will need:
8 oz. sausage meat	1 egg
chopped parsley	mixed herbs

1 Mix all ingredients together thoroughly.
2 If liked the finely chopped giblets of the poultry can be used.
3 This makes enough for a chicken. For a good-sized turkey use two to three times the quantity.

Veal stuffing

no cooking

you will need:
2 oz. shredded suet or melted margarine	4 oz. breadcrumbs
½ teaspoon mixed herbs	1 egg seasoning
grated rind and juice ½ lemon	2–3 teaspoons chopped parsley

1 Mix all the ingredients together thoroughly.
2 The cooked meat from the giblets can be added to make a rich stuffing, if wished.

3 Make two or three times this quantity for a large turkey.

Chestnut stuffing

cooking time: about 10 minutes

you will need:
1 lb. chestnuts	seasoning
2 tablespoons milk	2 oz. breadcrumbs
1 or 2 oz. margarine	

1 Boil the chestnuts for about 10 minutes, until soft.
2 Remove shells, and rub nuts through a sieve.
3 Mix with the rest of the ingredients.

Prune and sausage stuffing

cooking time: few minutes

you will need:
1 tablespoon oil or 1½ oz. margarine or butter	8 oz. sausage meat
1 small chopped onion	4 oz. prunes, soaked overnight
2 oz. mushrooms, sliced	2 oz. fresh white breadcrumbs pinch sage salt and pepper

1 Heat the oil, margarine, or butter and fry the onion and mushrooms for a few minutes.
2 Mix together the sausage meat, chopped prunes, breadcrumbs, sage and seasoning.
3 Add the onion and mushrooms and mix well.
4 This flavour is improved with a little 'taste' powder.

Bread sauce

cooking time: few minutes

you will need for 8 servings:
1 onion	4 oz. breadcrumbs
4 or 5 cloves, if liked	2–4 oz. margarine
1 pint milk	salt, pepper

1 Peel the onion and if using cloves, stick these firmly into onion.
2 Put into milk, together with other ingredients.
3 Slowly bring milk to the boil.
4 Remove from heat and stand in a warm place for as long as possible.
5 Just before the meal is ready, heat the sauce gently, beating it with a wooden spoon.
6 Remove onion before putting into sauce boat.

Pumpkin pie

cooking time: 45–55 minutes

you will need for 6–8 servings

8–10 oz. short crust pastry,* see page 72
approximately 1¼ lb. cooked pumpkin†
4 tablespoons milk
3 eggs
6 oz. sugar
grated rind and juice 1 lemon
½–1 teaspoon powdered ginger
½–1 teaspoon powdered cinnamon

*To line a 9-inch very deep flan ring or tin, or pie dish for greater depth.

†The pumpkin should be diced and steamed or cooked in very little water to keep it dry and to give as much flavour as possible—sieve or mash very thoroughly.

1 Roll out the pastry and line the ring or dish.
2 Blend together the sieved, cooked pumpkin, milk, eggs, sugar.
3 Beat very well, then add the lemon juice and rind and the spices.
4 Pour into the pastry case.
5 Bake for 20 minutes in a hot oven (425–450°F. –Gas Mark 6–7), then lower the heat to moderate (375°F.–Gas Mark 4) for a further 25–35 minutes.
6 Serve hot or cold, with cream or ice cream.

Variations

Meringue pumpkin pie – use only the egg yolks in the base and cook as above. Beat the egg whites until really stiff, fold in 3 oz sugar, if serving hot, and 6 oz. sugar if serving cold. To serve hot, replace in a moderate oven for 15 minutes; to serve cold, set meringue for at least an hour in a very cool oven.

Creamy pumpkin pie – as basic recipe, but increase milk to ¼ pint, and add ¼ pint cream. Set pastry as given for 15–20 minutes in a hot oven, then lower heat to a very moderate to make sure filling does not curdle.

Although this menu is suitable for a Christmas meal, it is also planned for an American Thanksgiving dinner, hence the pumpkin pie.

Christmas pudding

cooking time: 6–8 hours

you will need for 8 servings:

2 oz. flour, plain or self-raising
1 level teaspoon mixed spice
4 oz. brown sugar
4 oz. grated apple
1 small grated carrot
1 level teaspoon cinnamon
½ level teaspoon nutmeg
4 oz. mixed candied peel
4 oz. chopped blanched almonds
1 tablespoon golden syrup or black treacle
4 oz. fine breadcrumbs
4 oz. shredded or grated suet or melted margarine
1 lb. mixed dried fruit – 8 oz. raisins, 4 oz. sultanas, 4 oz. currants
grated rind and juice 1 large lemon
2 eggs
¼ pint stout, ale, beer or milk, or use nearly ¼ pint of these and 2 tablespoons rum

1 Mix all the ingredients thoroughly together.
2 Stir well and leave the mixture for 24 hours to mature.
3 Press into a large basin and cover with greased paper.
4 Cover, if wished, with a paste made from 6 oz. flour and water to give a firm dough; this keeps the pudding very dry.
5 Steam or boil for 6–8 hours.
6 Remove the damp covers and when cold put on dry paper.
7 Steam for a further 2–4 hours before serving.

Cream sauce

Whipped thick cream makes one of the most delicious sauces to serve with Christmas pudding. Lighten, as page 7, with egg white, adding vanilla.

Variations

With brandy – instead of vanilla, the cream can be flavoured with a few drops of brandy and a very small amount of grated lemon or orange rind.

Sherry cream – beat 2 egg yolks and 2 oz. sugar over hot water until thick and fluffy. As they thicken, add 2 tablespoons sherry, allow to cool, beating from time to time, and stir into ¼ pint of lightly whipped thick cream.

Tomato soup

See menu, page 36, but use half quantities for four people.

As a change, make this a clear tomato soup by using extra water or stock instead of milk or cream.

Casserole of guinea fowl and prunes

cooking time: about 2 hours

you will need for 4 servings:

1 guinea fowl	1 small cabbage
little seasoned flour	4 oz. stoned prunes
1 oz. dripping or fat	salt, black pepper
1 large onion	1 wineglass red wine
4 oz. pickled pork	4 smoked sausages

1 Truss bird neatly and roll in seasoned flour, brown all over in hot fat and remove from pan.
2 Fry onion and pickled pork until golden.
3 Shred and wash cabbage.
4 Put a thick layer of cabbage in bottom of casserole, mixing in onion, pickled pork and most of the prunes, season well with salt and pepper.
5 Place the bird on this and cover with the remaining cabbage.
6 Season again, pour over red wine and lay smoked sausages and remaining prunes on top.
7 Place lid on casserole and cook in moderate oven (375°F.–Gas Mark 4) for about 2 hours, or until bird is tender, adding more wine if required.

Variation

Casserole of duck – duck can be used in place of guinea fowl with the prunes. It is advisable to fry well to remove excess fat from the bird.

Golden apple pie

cooking time: 40 minutes

you will need for 4–6 servings:

8 oz. sweet short crust pastry, see page 72	apricot jam

For filling:

4 grated medium-sized cooking apples	2 eggs
rind 1 orange	3 level tablespoons castor sugar
1 oz. melted butter	

To serve:

cream or custard	meringue, optional

1 Grate the apples into a basin, add orange rind.
2 Mix in butter, eggs and sugar, blend well.
3 Roll out pastry on a lightly floured board and line a 9-inch pie plate, leaving sufficient pastry to decorate the top of the pie.
4 Decorate the edge of the pie shell and spread base with apricot jam.
5 Pour apple mixture into pie shell.
6 Roll out remaining pastry, cut into strips and place on top to form a lattice design.
7 Bake in centre of a moderately hot oven (400°F.–Gas Mark 5) for 40 minutes, covering top if it appears to be browning too quickly.
8 Serve with cream or custard, or a meringue, see page 24, may be placed on top, and cooked as page 24, use yolks only for apple mixture and whites with 2–4 oz. sugar for topping.

Creamy French onion soup

cooking time: 30 minutes

you will need for 4 servings:

6 medium-sized onions	salt, pepper
	1½ pints milk
2 oz. butter	2 oz. fine semolina
1 tablespoon flour	1 tablespoon cream, optional
½ pint boiling water	

To garnish:
grated Gruyère or Cheddar cheese

1 Cut onions into wafer thin rings then cut each ring across.
2 Fry gently in butter until pale gold.
3 Add the flour and stir well.
4 Slowly add the boiling water and stir with a wooden spoon until the mixture is smooth and even.
5 Season with salt and pepper.
6 Lower the heat and cook for 10 minutes in order to reduce the mixture.
7 Stir again, adding the milk slowly, and shower in the fine semolina.
8 Simmer very gently for 15 minutes or until the onions are soft.
9 A tablespoon of cream may be added to the soup after it is removed from the heat; or it can be topped with grated Gruyère or Cheddar cheese.

Variation

Brown French onion soup – fry the onions in the butter, omit the flour and semolina. Use 2 pints brown stock, simmer until onions are tender, top with slices of French bread and grated cheese.

Stuffed pigeons

cooking time: 1 hour

you will need for 4 servings:

2 large or 4 small pigeons	little fat
2 or 4 slices of bread or toast	few mushrooms

For sauce:

1 shallot	1 tablespoon meat jelly, when available
2 mushrooms	
½ oz. butter	4 tablespoons sherry
½ pint brown sauce, see right	

For stuffing:

4 tablespoons milk	2 oz. ham or bacon
1 thick slice bread, without crusts	1 small sprig parsley
2 shallots	hearts and livers of pigeons
2 mushrooms	seasoning

To garnish:

mushrooms	watercress
few cooked carrots	

1 First make the sauce by frying sliced shallot and mushrooms in hot butter, then add brown sauce and meat jelly.
2 Simmer very gently for 20 minutes, then add sherry, strain sauce if wished.
3 Make stuffing by pouring hot milk over bread, beat until smooth.
4 Chop all ingredients, including hearts and livers and add to bread mixture. Season.
5 Stuff pigeons with this.
6 Arrange birds on slices of bread or toast and cover with fat.
7 Bake near top of hot oven (450°F.–Gas Mark 7) for 30–35 minutes, adding mushrooms after 15 minutes.
8 Lift on to hot dish with bread underneath each pigeon, pour over some of the sauce.
9 Garnish with mushrooms, few cooked carrots, watercress, and serve rest of sauce separately.

Brown sauce

you will need:

1–2 oz. fat or dripping	½ pint brown stock
1 oz. flour	seasoning

1 Heat fat or dripping; a sliced onion and carrot can be fried in this, if wished.
2 Add flour, brown lightly, but do not burn.
3 Gradually stir in liquid, bring to boil, stir until thick and smooth. Season.

Variation

Madeira sauce – this is based on a brown sauce; but instead of ½ pint brown stock, use half stock and half Madeira wine. This is excellent with tongue or ham.

White sauce

This is made by the same method as brown sauce, except 1 oz. magarine or butter, 1 oz. flour, ½ pint milk are used for a coating sauce. Heat the margarine or butter, stir in the flour away from the heat, cook for several minutes being very careful that the flour does not burn. Remove from the heat, gradually stir in the milk bring to the boil and cook until thick and smooth. Season well.

Golden mallow apple pie

cooking time: 20–25 minutes

you will need for 4–6 servings:

6 oz. short crust or sweet short crust pastry, see page 72	2 oz. butter
	4 oz. soft brown sugar
1½ lb. cooking apples	½ level teaspoon cinnamon

To decorate:
4 oz. pink and white marshmallows

1 Make pastry, roll out and line an 8-inch pie plate.

2 Bake 'blind' in a hot oven (425–450°F.–Gas Mark 6–7) for approximately 20 minutes, until crisp and golden brown.
3 Peel, core and slice apples.
4 Melt butter in a pan, then add sugar, cinnamon and apples.
5 Cover pan and simmer gently until fruit is tender, but not broken and pulpy.
6 Turn into pie case and cover the top with halved marshmallows.
7 Toast lightly under a medium grill for about 1–2 minutes, or return to very low oven to melt marshmallows.

Lobster

no cooking

you will need for 4 servings:

2 small or 1 large cooked lobster	mixed salad mayonnaise

1 Split lobster, removing veins.
2 Crack claws, take out meat from these, and from body.
3 Either arrange neatly in the half shells with salad round, or pile in centre of salad.
4 Garnish with small claws and serve with mayonnaise.

Variations

Mornay – mix the lobster meat with ½ pint hot cheese sauce, see page 46. Pile into individual dishes or shells.

Au gratin – mix with cheese sauce, top with breadcrumbs, grated cheese and butter, brown under grill.

Americaine – mix lobster meat with fresh tomato purée, brandy, seasoning, little chopped onion or garlic and heat gently, pile back into shells.

Roast game

In the autumn there is a very wide variety of game from which to choose. Although it is expensive, it is very delicious. Grouse, pheasant and partridge are the most easily obtainable.

Young game

1 Roast in a hot oven (425–450°F.–Gas Mark 6–7).
2 Since game is inclined to dry, keep very well covered with fat during cooking.
3 Allow the following cooking times:
   Grouse – approximately 45–55 minutes, according to size.
   Pheasant – 15 minutes per lb. and 15 minutes over.
   Partridge – approximately 30 minutes.

Older game

The recipe for beef casserole, Burgundy beef in red wine, see page 83, is a very good basis for a casserole of game.

The usual accompaniments to game are: Bread sauce, see page 37, and/or red currant jelly.

Game chips – wafer thin slices of potato, fried until crisp, which can be bought in packets and re-heated.
Watercress or a green salad.

Fried crumbs – make rather coarse breadcrumbs and fry in hot fat or butter until tender.
Serve with thickened gravy or Venison sauce, see below.

Venison sauce

cooking time: 30 minutes

you will need:

1 onion	2 tablespoons cold water
6–8 cloves	
½ pint old ale	2 anchovies
1 tablespoon vinegar	seasoning

1 Peel onion and stick it with cloves.
2 Put the ale, vinegar and water into a pan.
3 Add the onion and cloves and the anchovies.
4 Season with salt and pepper and simmer for ½ hour.
5 Strain before serving.

Blackberry roly poly

cooking time: 40–45 minutes

you will need for 4–6 servings:
For pastry:
8 oz. plain flour
1 level teaspoon
  baking powder
½ level teaspoon salt
2 oz. butter
1 oz. castor sugar
For filling:
12 oz. fresh
  blackberries
For topping:
beaten egg or milk
2 level teaspoons
  castor sugar

2 level teaspoons
  finely grated lemon
  rind
5–6 tablespoons cold
  milk to mix

2–3 oz. castor sugar

1 oz. butter

1 Sieve flour, baking powder and salt and rub in butter finely.
2 Stir in sugar and lemon rind.
3 Mix to a soft dough with milk, knead lightly on a floured board till smooth, then roll out into a rectangle, approximately 12-inches × 10-inches.
4 Turn dough over then cover with 10 oz. fruit to within 1 inch of edges.
5 Moisten edges with water, sprinkle fruit with sugar then roll up like a Swiss roll, starting from one of the shorter sides.
6 Press joins well together to seal then transfer to a heatproof dish.
7 Make three slits on top of roll, brush with egg or milk and sprinkle with sugar.
8 Dot small pieces of butter on the top, pour three tablespoons water into the dish then add remaining blackberries.
9 Bake in the centre of a hot oven (425–450°F.– Gas Mark 6–7) for 15 minutes then reduce to moderate (375°F.–Gas Mark 4) for 25–30 minutes.
10 Serve hot with cream or custard.

Variation
Blackberry and apple roly poly – use 8 oz. good cooking apples, and 8 oz. blackberries. Peel and slice the apples very thinly before using.

Supper Parties

Supper party menus are a pleasure to prepare because they can be as formal or as informal as one wishes. I have supplied recipes to suit the various occasions for which guests may be invited to supper.

Food for a supper party

This can be very much like a dinner party, but generally fewer courses are served. Two fairly sustaining courses are considered by most people to be ample, or a main dish with cheese and fruit to follow.
Because supper parties are informal, and one tends to linger over serving and eating the food, take care to choose dishes that are 'good-tempered' about waiting.

Fried prawns with sauce

cooking time: approximately 35 minutes

you will need for 4 servings:
approximately 36 large
  prawns

oil or fat for frying

For batter:
2 oz. flour
pinch salt
1 egg

1 dessertspoon oil
just under ¼ pint milk

1 Coat the prawns in a thin batter made by beating all the batter ingredients together.
2 Fry in hot oil or fat until crisp and brown.
3 Serve with sweet sour sauce.

With chicken – tiny cubes of chicken, which need not be coated but just fried, can be served in the sweet sour sauce.

With lobster – lobster meat can be cut into large pieces and actually put in the sweet sour sauce.

White fish – white uncooked fish can be cut in neat cubes, coated, fried and served with sweet sour sauce.

Sweet sour sauce

cooking time: 5–10 minutes

you will need for 4 servings:

2 tablespoons vinegar	2–3 oz. chopped,
1½ tablespoons sugar	canned pineapple
½ tablespoon tomato	OR, for a more spicy
ketchup or purée	flavour, 2–3 oz.
1 dessertspoon	finely chopped
cornflour	mustard pickles
1½ teaspoons soy	2 oz. very finely
sauce	chopped onions,
½ pint water	spring onions or
salt	pickled onions
2 teaspoons oil	

1 Blend vinegar, sugar, tomato ketchup or purée, cornflour, soy sauce with the water.
2 Put into a saucepan and cook until thick.
3 Add the salt and oil and continue cooking for a few minutes.
4 Lastly stir in the pineapple or mustard pickles, and onion.

Pineapple whip flan

cooking time: 25 minutes

you will need for 4–5 servings:
flan pastry made with 4 oz. flour, etc., see page 22
For filling:

1 large can crushed	2 teaspoons lemon
pineapple	juice
1 teaspoon arrowroot	1 egg
or cornflour	4 oz. can cream, or
2 oz. castor sugar	fresh thick cream

To decorate:

few whole skinned	glacé cherries
almonds	

1 Roll out the pastry to fit a 7-inch flan ring.
2 Bake 'blind', see page 50, in the centre of a moderately hot oven (400°F.–Gas Mark 5), for 20 minutes.
3 Drain the pineapple and place in a saucepan.
4 Blend the arrowroot or cornflour with the pineapple juice and add to the fruit.
5 Bring to the boil and simmer for 2–3 minutes.
6 Remove from the heat and add 1 oz. of the sugar and the lemon juice.
7 Beat in the egg yolk.
8 Return to the heat and cook gently until the mixture thickens.
9 Allow to cool, then put into the flan case.
10 Whip the cream until stiff and spread over the pineapple mixture.

11 Make a meringue, see page 24, with the egg white and remaining sugar and place on top of the flan, covering the filling completely.
12 Decorate with almonds and cherries and bake for 5 minutes in the same oven as before. Serve immediately.

Eggs Florentine

cooking time: 5–15 minutes plus cooking of spinach and eggs

you will need for 4 hors-d'oeuvre servings:
for 2 main course servings:

8–12 oz. creamed	½ pint white sauce,
spinach	see page 40
4 hardboiled eggs	2–3 oz. grated cheese

1 Arrange the spinach at the bottom of an oven-proof dish.
2 Top with the halved eggs and the sauce.
3 Sprinkle with grated cheese and heat for a few minutes under the grill or in the oven.

Salmon mayonnaise

cooking time: see method

you will need for 4 servings:

4 cutlets salmon	butter or oil
5–6 oz. each	seasoning
OR 1½ lb. piece of	mayonnaise, page 44
salmon	mixed salad

To garnish:
lemon

1 There are several ways of cooking salmon. Either wrap each steak in buttered foil, season lightly and bake for approximately 20 minutes in a moderately hot oven (400°F.–Gas Mark 5).
2 Or wrap all the steaks or pieces of fish together in buttered or oiled greaseproof paper and tie firmly, put into a pan of cold water, bring the water steadily up to the boil.
3 For the small amount of salmon, remove the pan from the heat, but leave the salmon in the water until cold.
4 For the large piece of salmon, allow 7–10 minutes per lb., with the water gently simmering, then lift out of the water at the end of the cooking time.
5 Serve with mayonnaise and salad, garnish with lemon wedges.

Variation

Fish mayonnaise – use cutlets of turbot, hake, fresh haddock, or pieces of skate, cook and serve in place of salmon. In order to give more colour to the dish, the mayonnaise can be flavoured with a little anchovy essence.

Salmon and fish mould

In order to make a more economical dish, use half each of white fish and salmon and cook as given, then flake the fish coarsely, blend with some mayonnaise and chopped parsley. Put into a mould or basin, leave for a while to make a neat shape, turn out and serve on a bed of lettuce.

Mayonnaise

no cooking

you will need:

1 egg yolk
good pinch salt, pepper and mustard
4 tablespoons–¼ pint oil

1 dessertspoon vinegar
1 dessertspoon warm water

1 Put the egg yolk and seasonings into a basin.
2 Gradually beat in the oil, drop by drop, stirring all the time until the mixture is thick. When you find it creamy, stop adding oil, for too much will make the mixture curdle.
3 Beat in the vinegar gradually, then the warm water.
4 Use when fresh.
  If using an electric blender, put egg, seasoning and vinegar into goblet. Switch on for a few seconds, then pour oil in steadily.

Variation

Tartare sauce – add approximately 1 tablespoon chopped parsley, 1 tablespoon chopped gherkins, 1 dessertspoon chopped capers to the above mayonnaise. Quantities can be altered for personal taste.

Eastern cream

cooking time: few minutes

you will need for 4 servings:

3 eggs
6 oz. castor sugar
juice and rind 1 lemon
3 tablespoons syrup from jar stem ginger

¼ pint thick cream
2 teaspoons gelatine
little hot water
2 oz. preserved stem ginger

1 Separate the egg yolks from the whites.
2 Add the sugar and lemon rind to the yolks, place over a saucepan of hot water and whisk until very thick and much lighter in colour.
3 Slowly add the lemon juice and ginger syrup, whisking between each addition to ensure that the mixture remains thick.
4 Beat the cream to piping consistency, fold into the egg mixture.
5 Dissolve the gelatine in the hot water and stir into the mixture.
6 Whisk the egg whites until stiff and fold quickly through the mixture, stir in the chopped ginger.
7 Allow to stand in a cool place until nearly set, then divide into sundae glasses.

Salmon steak mornay

cooking time: 30 minutes

you will need for 4 servings:

1 onion
3 oz. butter or margarine
4 salmon steaks
1 pint fish stock or water
1 oz. flour

2 tablespoons grated Parmesan cheese
2 teaspoons lemon juice
1 tablespoon cream or top of milk
salt and pepper

1 Chop the onion.
2 Put half the butter into a saucepan and, when melted, fry the onion and salmon quickly on both sides.
3 Pour in the stock or water, cover and simmer gently for 20 minutes.
4 Meanwhile melt the remaining butter in another saucepan, add the flour and cook for 2 minutes.
5 When the fish is cooked, place on a hot serving dish and keep warm.
6 Strain the stock over the flour and butter and stir until boiling.
7 Simmer for 5 minutes, then add the cheese, lemon juice and cream, re-heat, but do not boil.

8 Season to taste and pour the sauce over the fish.
9 Serve with green salad or cooked peas and green and cucumber salad.

Variations

Salmon steak au gratin – cover top of dish with breadcrumbs, grated cheese and brown under grill before serving.

White fish mornay – use cutlets of white fish instead of salmon.

Plate pie

cooking time: 40 minutes

you will need for 4–6 servings:
8 oz. short crust   1 lb. fruit
  pastry, see page 72   sugar to taste

1 Make the pastry and roll out half into a neat round.
2 Put this over a 7-inch pie plate.
3 Cover with fruit, adding sugar and a few drops of water.
4 Roll out the second half of pastry and put over the top of the fruit.
5 Press the edges together and cut off surplus pastry, cutting away from you to prevent the pastry from stretching.
6 Flake the edges together and brush the top of the pie with a little water or milk and make a fine slit in the centre to allow the steam to escape.
7 Bake in the centre of a hot oven (425°F.–Gas Mark 6) for 20 minutes, then lower the heat to moderate (375°F.–Gas Mark 4) for a further 20 minutes, until the pastry is cooked.

Variations

Fruit pie

cooking time: 35–45 minutes

you will need for 4–6 servings:
1–1½ lb. fruit   5–6 oz. pastry, short,
very little water   flaky or puff, see
sugar to taste   pages 72, 64 and 70

1 Put the fruit into a pie dish with a small amount of water and sugar to taste.
2 If there is not enough fruit, put in a pie support or an egg cup.
3 Roll out the pastry to the shape of the pie dish,

but make it 1–1½ inches larger all round.
4 Cut off a long narrow strip.
5 Moisten the edge of the pie dish with a little water and press the strip of pastry to the rim.
6 Lift up the pastry with the air of the rolling pin and lay it over the top of the pie.
7 Press the edges together and flake the pastry with a knife. Brush with a little water.
8 Shake over a little sugar.
9 Bake in the centre of a hot oven (425–450°F.– Gas Mark 6–7) for short crust pastry or a very hot oven (450–475°F.–Gas Mark 7–8) for flaky or puff pastry, until the top of the pie is golden brown.
10 Turn the heat to moderate (375°F.–Gas Mark 4) for a further 15 minutes, to make sure the fruit is cooked.
11 It is advisable to stand the pie dish on a baking tray, in case any juice boils out in cooking.

Fruit tarts

If preferred, make individual tarts. Line fairly deep patty tins with pastry, fill with fruit and a little sugar, (no water), and top with pastry, sealing edges as described above. Bake for approximately 10 minutes towards the top of a hot oven (425–450°F.–Gas Mark 6–7), then for another 15 minutes at a lower heat to make sure the fruit is cooked through.

Mincemeat tart

Put mincemeat into either the large plate pie or the small tarts and bake as fruit.

Avocado and grapefruit salad

no cooking

you will need for 4 servings:
1 large or 2 small   little lemon juice
  avocado pears   crisp lettuce
1 large or 2 small
  grapefruit

1 Remove the pieces of flesh from both the grapefruit and avocado, keeping these as neat as possible.
2 You may be able to strip the peel from the avocado, if it is the right degree of ripeness.
3 Sprinkle the slices of avocado with lemon juice to keep them white, and arrange with the grapefruit on crisp lettuce.

Fish mornay flan

cooking time: 30–40 minutes

you will need for 4 servings:

4 oz. short or cheese crust pastry, see pages 72 and 10.
For filling:

cheese sauce made with:
12 tablespoons milk
½ oz. margarine
½ oz. flour
salt, pepper
3 oz. grated cheese

8–10 oz. cooked white fish OR medium-sized can tuna fish or salmon
To garnish:
parsley
lemon butterflies

1 Line 7-inch flan or sandwich tin with pastry and bake 'blind' for approximately 20 minutes in centre of hot oven (425–450°F.–Gas Mark 6–7) if using short crust, or moderately hot oven (400°F.–Gas Mark 5) with cheese pastry, allowing little longer cooking time.
2 Make cheese sauce, add fish, put into flan.
3 Garnish with parsley and lemon butterflies.
4 Serve hot or cold with green salad or Duchesse potatoes, see below, and peas.

Variation
Creamed fish flan – use white instead of cheese sauce, adding a little cream, chopped parsley and diced gherkins.

Duchesse potatoes

cooking time: 20 minutes

you will need for 4 servings:

1–2 egg yolks
2 oz. butter

1 lb. mashed, sieved potatoes
seasoning

1 Beat egg yolks and butter into potatoes.
2 Season well.
3 Pipe into large rosettes on a greased tin or dish, bake at 400°F.–Gas Mark 5.

Plum meringue pudding

cooking time: 1½ hours

you will need for 4–6 servings:

1 lb. cooking plums, stoned and halved
juice and rind ½ orange
3 oz. sugar
½ pint water
6 oz. day-old white bread, cut into ½-inch cubes

2 oz. butter
2 egg yolks
1 level teaspoon cinnamon
meringue made with 2 egg whites, see page 24

1 Stew the prepared plums gently with the orange juice and rind, sugar and water.
2 Drain the fruit and pour the hot syrup over the bread cubes.
3 Soak for 7–10 minutes.
4 Cream the butter, beat in the egg yolks and soaked bread cubes.
5 Add the drained fruit and the cinnamon.
6 Put into a 2-pint greased, ovenproof dish and bake in the centre of a moderate oven (375°F. –Gas Mark 4) for 30–35 minutes or till set.
7 Make the meringue and pile on top of the pudding.
8 Return to cool oven (225–250°F.–Gas Mark 0–½) until meringue is pale gold, approximately 1 hour.

Fish and mushrooms with bamboo shoots

cooking time: 10–12 minutes

you will need for 4 servings:

1 lb. firm white fish
little diced ginger, optional
fat or oil for frying
2 tiny, chopped spring onions

2–3 oz. mushrooms
1 oz. bamboo shoots
extra soy or soya sauce
2–3 tablespoons sherry

For coating:

1 tablespoon sherry
1 tablespoon soy or soya sauce
good pinch salt, pepper

1 level dessertspoon cornflour
1 egg white

To serve:
fried rice
  see page 51

crispy fried noodles,
  see page 51

1 Cut the fish into 1-inch cubes.
2 Blend the ingredients for coating, and thoroughly coat the fish.
3 Fry in hot oil or fat until golden brown, put on dish and keep hot.
4 Add the spring onions, ginger, if liked, sliced mushrooms, sliced bamboo shoots, extra soy or soya sauce and sherry to a little oil in the pan and heat thoroughly for a few minutes.
5 Pour over the fish and serve with fried rice or crispy fried noodles.

Variations

With sole – can be served in a similar way, but the fillets should be cut into 2-inch lengths, coated as before and fried.

With cucumber and nuts – finely diced cucumber and a few finely chopped nuts can be added to the mushrooms, to pour over the fish.

Fresh cherry vacherin

cooking time: 3 hours

you will need for 4–6 servings:

meringue made with 2 egg whites	2 tablespoons cherry brandy, optional
12 oz. fresh cherries	1 large block vanilla ice cream

1 Make the meringue, see page 24.
2 Place in a piping bag or syringe fitted with a meringue star pipe, and on a sheet of oiled greasproof paper, pipe a 'catherine wheel' about 8-inch in diameter.
3 Round the edge of the 'wheel' pipe a border of rosettes.
4 Set in a cool oven (225–250°F.–Gas Mark 0–½), see page 24.
5 When cool, place the meringue base on a serving dish.
6 Stone 8 oz. of cherries and if using cherry brandy, let them soak in this for a while.
7 Fill the centre of the meringue base with the cherries, place spoonfuls of ice cream on the top.
8 Decorate with remaining whole cherries.

Hot grapefruit

cooking time: 5 or 10–12 minutes

you will need for 4 servings:

2 grapefruit	little mixed spice
1 oz. butter	OR
1 tablespoon brown sugar	little sherry
	4 glacé cherries

1 Halve the grapefruit and loosen flesh from the skin.
2 Spread with butter and sugar and sprinkle over the spice or sherry.
3 Heat for 5 minutes under the grill, or 10–12 minutes in a moderately hot oven (400°F.–Gas Mark 5).
4 Top with the glacé cherries.

Bacon crumb pie

cooking time: 20 minutes

you will need for 4 servings:

6 oz. back rashers bacon	2 hardboiled eggs
2 oz. margarine	¼ pint stock
3 oz. breadcrumbs	salt, pepper
8 oz. cooked, sliced carrots	2–3 tomatoes

To garnish:
parsley

1 Remove rinds from bacon and cut into fairly small pieces.
2 Fry lightly and remove from pan.
3 Melt margarine in pan and toss the breadcrumbs in it.
4 Place layers of bacon, carrots, and sliced eggs in a pie dish, pour over well-seasoned stock and cover with breadcrumbs.
5 Bake in a moderately hot oven (400°F.–Gas Mark 5) for 20 minutes.
6 For the last 5 minutes cooking time lay sliced skinned tomatoes across top of the crumbs.
7 Garnish with chopped parsley, and serve with baked mushrooms and scalloped potatoes.

Scalloped potatoes

cooking time: 1–2 hours

you will need for 4 servings:

1–1½ lb. peeled old or new potatoes	2 oz. butter
seasoning	approximately ½ pint milk

1 Slice the potatoes very thinly and arrange in a baking dish. Season each layer and add a little of the butter and milk.
2 Either bake for 1 hour in a moderately hot oven (400°F.–Gas Mark 5) or for 1½–2 hours in a very slow oven (250–275°F.–Gas Mark ½–1).

Baked mushrooms

cooking time: 15 minutes

you will need for 4 servings:

8 oz. mushrooms	2 oz. butter

1 Prepare the mushrooms.
2 Put into a shallow dish topped with butter, and cover with foil.
3 Bake for about 15 minutes in a moderately hot oven (400°F.–Gas Mark 5).

Austrian cheese cakes

cooking time: about 10 minutes

you will need for 4–6 servings:
For almond pastry:

4 oz. butter	salt, pepper
6 oz. flour	paprika
2 oz. ground almonds	tabasco sauce
3 oz. grated cheese	1 tablespoon water
1 egg yolk	egg to glaze

1 Rub butter into flour, add almonds, nearly all the cheese, egg yolk, seasoning, paprika, tabasco sauce, and water.
2 Bind to a firm dough.
3 Roll out about ⅛-inch thick and cut into rounds.
4 Brush with beaten egg, sprinkle with remaining cheese and bake in a moderately hot oven (400°F–Gas Mark 5) for approximately 10 minutes until golden brown.
5 When cool, sandwich together with the following filling.

For cheesecake filling:

1½ oz. grated cheese	pepper, salt, paprika
¼ pint milk	¼ oz. butter
1 teaspoon arrowroot	few drops tabasco
1 egg	sauce

1 Mix together cheese, milk, arrowroot, egg yolk and seasoning.
2 Cook gently without boiling, stirring all the time.
3 Add butter and cool.
4 Whisk egg white and fold in with tabasco sauce.

Haddock casserole

cooking time: 35–40 minutes

you will need for 4–6 servings:

1½ lb. haddock*	1 bay leaf
few shrimps or prawns	½ pint milk
squeeze lemon juice	¾ oz. cornflour
4 tablespoons white wine	cooked carrots
butter	2 tablespoons cooked peas
salt, pepper	

To garnish:

grated nutmeg	parsley

*Other white fish could be used.

1 Wash the fish and cut into fairly large portions.
2 Place in a baking dish with the drained shrimps,

a squeeze of lemon juice, white wine, few knobs of butter, seasoning and bay leaf.
3 Cover and bake in a slow oven (300°F.–Gas Mark 2) until the fish is tender, about 25 minutes.
4 Remove the bay leaf, then carefully strain off the liquor.
5 Put the fish into a casserole and keep hot.
6 Make the liquor up to ¾ pint with milk, blend the cornflour smoothly with a little of the liquor and put the rest on to heat.
7 Add the mixed cornflour and boil for 3 minutes, stirring constantly.
8 Remove from the heat, add a few cooked carrots and the cooked peas, then pour over the fish.
9 Sprinkle with a little grated nutmeg and garnish with parsley.
10 Serve with creamed, Duchesse or scalloped potatoes, see below and pages 46 and 47, cauliflower and beans.

Creamed potatoes

Beautifully creamed potatoes blend with most dishes.

1 Boil the potatoes in hot salted water, not too quickly.
2 When cooked, strain and break first with a fork or potato masher, or sieve.
3 Heat 1 oz. butter and 2–3 tablespoons milk, to each 1 lb. of cooked potatoes, in a separate pan.
4 Pour on to the smooth potatoe purée, add extra seasoning, blend slowly with a wooden spoon to begin with, and then beat until like a thick white cream.

Love apple pie

cooking time: 30 minutes

you will need for 6 servings:

6 oz. short crust pastry, see page 72	2 teaspoons lemon juice
2¼ lb. cooking apples, peeled	6 oz. sugar
7 dessertspoons tomato ketchup	3 oz. flour
	½ teaspoon ground cinnamon
	6 oz. butter

1 Make short crust pastry and line a pie dish, bake 'blind' for 10 minutes in hot oven.

2 Cook apples until soft, then drain off excess juice, blend in tomato ketchup and lemon juice, (if apples are very tart add a little sugar) and leave to cool.

3 Combine sugar, flour and cinnamon and rub in butter until thoroughly mixed.

4 Fill pie dish with apples, top with sugar mixture and bake in moderate oven (375°F.–Gas Mark 4) for 30 minutes.

Variation

With ice cream – serve warm with vanilla ice cream, if liked.

Fish scallops

cooking time: 20–25 minutes

you will need for 4 hors-d'oeuvre servings:

for 2 main course servings:

12 oz. white fish	8 oz. creamed
salt	potatoes, optional
seasoning	1 oz. butter
white sauce made	
with:	
1 oz. butter	¼ pint milk
1 oz. flour	

To garnish:

parsley	lemon

1 Cook the fish in salted water until just tender.

2 Flake fish, make the white sauce, stir in the fish with 2 tablespoons of the fish stock.

3 Season very well.

4 If using mashed potato, pipe a border round the edge of four scallop shells or individual dishes.

5 Top with extra butter, fill with the creamy fish mixture and brown under the grill.

6 Garnish with chopped parsley and serve with wedges of lemon.

Variations

Fish scallops mornay – add 2–3 oz. grated cheese to the white sauce.

Creamy fish scallops – add a little cream instead of fish stock.

Au gratin fish scallops – top the fish mixture with breadcrumbs, grated cheese, brown under grill.

Piquant fish scallops – add chopped olives and gherkins to the sauce.

Shellfish scallops – use prawns, shrimps, flaked lobster or crab, instead of white fish.

Casserole of liver and apples

cooking time: 1 hour 40 minutes

you will need for 4 servings:

1 lb. calves liver	2 medium-sized
1 oz. flour	cooking apples
salt, pepper	2 medium-sized
1 teaspoon dry	onions, sliced
mustard	6 rashers streaky
2 oz. fat	bacon
	½ pint water

1 Cut liver into thin slices.

2 Mix together flour, salt, pepper and mustard, and coat the slices of liver.

3 Brown liver lightly in heated fat.

4 Fill a greased casserole dish with alternate layers of liver, sliced and cored apples and onions, then top with pieces of bacon.

5 Add water. Cover casserole and cook in the centre of a moderate oven (355°F.–Gas Mark 4) for 1½ hours, removing lid for the last 20 minutes.

6 Serve with creamy mashed potatoes, made mustard, and spinach.

Coffee cornflake flan

cooking time: 20 minutes

you will need for 4 servings:

4 oz. short or sweet	1 heaped teaspoon
crust pastry, see	soluble coffee
page 72	powder
little jam	1 level tablespoon
2 oz. margarine or	syrup
butter	2 oz. cornflakes
1 oz. sugar	

To decorate:

¼ pint thick cream	crystallised violet
pinch soluble coffee	petals
powder	angelica

1 Line 8-inch flan ring, sandwich tin or pie plate with the pastry.

2 Spread with jam.

3 Cream the margarine, sugar and coffee powder with the syrup.

4 Fold in sufficient cornflakes to absorb the mixture.

5 Pile into pastry case and bake in a moderate oven (375°F.–Gas Mark 4) for 20 minutes until crisp.

6 Decorate with whipped cream (to which coffee powder is added), violet petals and angelica leaves.

Grilled chicken

cooking time: about 15 minutes

you will need for 4 servings:

2 small spring chickens	butter
seasoning	tomatoes
	mushrooms

1 Halve the chickens down the centre, season well and brush with melted butter.
2 Put under a pre-heated grill and cook on both sides, basting well with butter, until brown.
3 Lower the heat and allow to cook more gently until tender.
4 Tomatoes and mushrooms can be put in the grill pan to cook at the same time.
5 Serve with green salad.

Variations

Devilled grilled chicken – blend a little curry powder, pinch cayenne pepper and about 1 tablespoon Worcestershire sauce to the melted butter used at stage 1.

Lemon grilled chicken – blend the finely grated rind of a lemon and 2 tablespoons lemon juice with the melted butter at stage 1.

Harlequin rice

cooking time: 50 minutes

you will need for 4–6 servings:

4 medium-sized onions	$\frac{1}{4}$ pint bottled apple juice OR stock OR
2 medium-sized tomatoes	$\frac{1}{4}$ pint water juice $\frac{1}{2}$ lemon
2 oz. butter or dripping	1 teaspoon sugar
1 teaspoon salt	$\frac{1}{2}$ clove garlic, crushed, optional
$\frac{1}{4}$ teaspoon pepper	$\frac{1}{2}$ teaspoon Worcestershire sauce
4 oz. long grain rice	

1 Slice onions and skin and slice tomatoes.
2 Brown in the fat.
3 Add remaining ingredients, pour into a casserole and cover.
4 Bake in a very moderate oven (350°F.–Gas Mark 3) for 50 minutes, until rice is tender.
5 Toss rice mixture lightly with a fork twice during last 20 minutes of cooking.

Gooseberry meringue pie

cooking time: 35 minutes

you will need for 4–6 servings:
6 oz. short crust pastry, see page 72

For filling:

1 lb. fresh gooseberries	$\frac{3}{4}$ oz. cornflour
4 oz. castor sugar	1 egg yolk
$\frac{1}{4}$ pint water	green colouring

For meringue:

1 egg white	2 oz. castor sugar

1 Line an 8-inch pie plate with pastry and bake 'blind', see below, for 20 minutes in a hot oven (425–450°F.–Gas Mark 6–7).
2 Stew the gooseberries gently in the sugar and water until tender.
3 Rub through a sieve and make quantity up to $\frac{3}{4}$ pint with water, if necessary. Cool.
4 Mix the cornflour with a little of the cold purée and put the rest on to heat.
5 Add mixed cornflour, stir until boiling, and boil 3 minutes stirring all the time.
6 Add egg yolk and cook without boiling for several minutes.
7 Colour with green colouring, if necessary.
8 Pour into pastry case.
9 Whisk the egg white until stiff and fold in the sugar.
10 Pipe the meringue in a lattice work design on top of the pie and brown in a moderate oven for 10–15 minutes (375°F.–Gas Mark 4). Serve hot.
11 If serving cold set meringue very slowly in a cool oven (225–250°F.–Gas Mark 0–1) for 1 hour.

To line a flan ring

Put the flan ring on to a baking tin turned upside down, this means the cooked pastry can slide off easily. Make the pastry, and in order to put it into the flan ring easily, lift over a rolling pin. Insert the pastry with the help of the rolling pin, then roll firmly over the top to give a neat edge.

To bake 'blind'

This means that the pastry should be baked without a filling. To weigh it down, put a piece of greased greaseproof paper or foil inside the pastry case, cover this with bread crusts or dry haricot beans. Bake for about 15 minutes in a hot oven, then remove beans and paper and return to the oven for a further 5–10 minutes to brown.

Chicken with walnuts

cooking time: about 10 minutes

you will need for 4 servings:

2 oz. walnuts
1 small onion
1 small red pepper
4 tablespoons oil
12 oz. cooked chicken
  cut in strips
½ pint stock
½ oz. cornflour
1 level teaspoon sugar

1 tablespoon soy sauce
2 tablespoons sherry
5 oz. can water
  chestnuts drained
  and sliced
To serve:
cooked rice OR
  crispy fried noodles.

1 Fry the coarsely broken walnuts, sliced onion and sliced red pepper in the oil, until the onion and pepper are tender, but not brown.
2 Stir in the chicken. Add the stock.
3 Mix the cornflour and sugar smoothly with the soy sauce, add to ingredients in pan and simmer gently for 3 minutes stirring constantly.
4 Add sherry and chestnuts and warm through.
5 Serve hot with cooked rice, either boiled or fried, or with crispy fried noodles.

Methods of cooking rice

For most savoury dishes choose a long grain rice.

Boiled rice

Method 1

To each 4 oz. rice allow 2 pints boiling salted water. Put in the rice, cook rapidly for approximately 14–15 minutes. Strain, rinse in boiling water, put on to flat trays in a cool oven to dry for a short time.

Method 2

Either use a cup measure or an oz. measure and allow 1 cup rice, 2 cups water; or 4 oz. rice, 8 oz. water. Put the rice, cold water, salt to taste, into a saucepan with a tightly fitting lid. Bring to the boil, stir briskly with a fork, put on the lid, lower the heat and simmer gently for 15 minutes. By this time the water will have been absorbed and every grain of rice cooked, but not sticky.

Fried rice

Boil the rice by either method, taking care not to overcook. Allow to dry, then put in hot oil or fat and cook until golden.

Crispy fried noodles

Cook the noodles in boiling salted water until just tender but not overcooked. Strain, dry well on kitchen paper or use a tea cloth. Heat in really hot oil until crisp and golden brown.

Pineapple meringue pie

cooking time: 30 minutes

you will need for 4–6 servings:

biscuit crumbs crust,
  see page 52

1×15 oz. can
  pineapple pieces
meringue made with 2 egg whites, see page 24

1 oz. cornflour
4 oz. castor sugar
2 egg yolks
1 oz. butter

1 Drain the pineapple pieces and make the liquid up to ½ pint with water.
2 Mix the cornflour, sugar and egg yolks smoothly with a little of the liquid and put the rest on to heat.
3 Add to the mixed cornflour.
4 Return to the pan, bring to the boil and boil 1 minute stirring all the time.
5 Remove from the heat and add the butter and pineapple pieces and mix well.
6 Pour into the pie crust.
7 Make the meringue and pipe or spoon on to the filled case and bake for approximately 30 minutes in a very moderate oven (325–350°F. –Gas Mark 2–3) until the meringue is lightly browned.
8 If wished, decorate with a few glacé cherries and angelica.

Variations

Apricot meringue pie – use a can of apricots in place of pineapple.
Apricot and lemon meringue pie – drain the syrup from a can of apricots, add the juice and very finely grated rind of a lemon, then enough water to make ½ pint.
Berry fruit meringue pie – use canned loganberries, raspberries or strawberries. If using fresh fruit, make a syrup of ½ pint water, 2–3 oz. sugar, and continue as basic recipe.

Biscuit crumbs crust

you will need:

8 oz. wholemeal biscuits	2 oz. castor sugar
	4 oz. margarine

1 Crush the biscuits finely, add sugar and melted margarine.
2 Press into a 9-inch pie dish, bringing mixture up the sides of the dish.
3 Bake for 15 minutes in a moderate oven (375°F.–Gas Mark 4) for extra crispness, or allow to set in refrigerator.

Spaghetti with tomato and red pepper sauce

cooking time: 1 hour

you will need for 8–12 hors-d'oeuvre servings:

for 4–6 main course servings:

2 tablespoons oil	hot water or stock
1 clove garlic	salt, pepper
1 onion, sliced	
1 lb. cooked, minced pork or beef	1 lb. spaghetti
	Parmesan or Gruyère cheese
1 lb. tomatoes	
1 sweet red pepper (capsicum)	green salad
2 tablespoons chopped parsley	

1 Start cooking the sauce first as it takes longer then the spaghetti. Heat the oil in a pan, brown the garlic, onion and pork.
2 Take out garlic, add chopped, skinned tomatoes, sliced red pepper and parsley.
3 Cook for 5 minutes before adding sufficient hot water or stock to make a sauce.
4 Add salt and pepper last.
5 Simmer until tomatoes are reduced to a pulp, stirring occasionally.
6 The longer you cook the better, but make sure the sauce does not become too dry – if making early in day to reheat, leave it a little moist.
7 Cook the spaghetti in the usual way, drain, and mix well with plenty of grated cheese, pile on large dish.
8 Pour the sauce over and serve extra cheese in a deep bowl, and green salad.

Green salad

To be correct, a green salad should have lettuce or endive, watercress, and/or mustard and cress; a little shredded green pepper. But many people like to add chopped celery and/or fennel, and thin strips of cucumber. Normally one does not add tomatoes, hard-boiled eggs, beetroot, etc.

Wash the salad greens, shake dry in a cloth or salad shaker. Break into convenient-sized pieces, and toss in oil and vinegar or French dressing, see page 28, just before serving so the crispness is not lost.

Mixed salad

Have a base of green salad as above. Add quartered hardboiled eggs, tomatoes, sliced or whole radishes. Diced beetroot should only be added at the last moment to prevent discoloration, although diced canned beetroot does not dye other ingredients in the same way as fresh.

Winter salad

Often lettuce are very expensive in winter and not very good, so use a base of cabbage or Brussels sprouts.

Other salad ingredients

A few shredded nasturtium leaves washed very well – use sparingly as rather hot.
Grated or diced celeriac.
Diced celery and celery leaves.
Grated raw swede, carrot, turnips when very young.
Cooked peas in a mild-flavoured French dressing.
Cooked French or runner beans.
Diced potatoes (apart from a potato salad).

Diced fruits – apples, bananas, pineapple.
Soft berry fruits.

Pavlova cake

cooking time: 4–5 hours

you will need for 4–6 servings:

3 egg whites	½ teaspoon cornflour
6 oz. castor sugar	½ teaspoon vinegar
½ teaspoon vanilla essence	filling

1 Beat the egg whites until stiff.
2 Continue beating, gradually adding the sugar.
3 Beat until sugar is dissolved and the mixture is standing well in peaks.
4 Fold in vanilla, cornflour and vinegar.
5 Spread mixture in a 6–7-inch circle on grease-proof paper, on a baking sheet, making the sides higher than the centre to form a shell to hold the filling.
6 Put into cool oven (225–250°F.–Gas Mark 0–½) and bake for 4–5 hours.
7 The Pavlova should be crisp and very slightly tinted, yet soft and of marshmallow consistency in centre.
8 Cool and store in tin until required.

Fillings

With fruit and cream – whipped, flavoured thick cream with any kind of canned or fresh fruit piled on top and decorated with maraschino cherries or angelica.

With lemon curd – lemon curd made with egg yolks.

Rice with chicken livers (Risotto)

cooking time: 35 minutes

you will need for 8–12 hors-d'oeuvre servings:

for 4–6 main course servings:

1 small onion	3 pints chicken stock
4 oz. mushrooms	seasoning
6–8 chicken livers*	little Marsala,
3 oz. butter	optional
12 oz. Patna rice	Parmesan cheese
small sweet red pepper (capsicum)	

*More if liked.

1 Toss the chopped onion, mushrooms and chicken livers in hot butter in a saucepan.
2 Add the rice and finely chopped red pepper and cook for about 10 minutes, stirring very well.
3 Add the chicken stock, stirring all the time, and then cook steadily until the liquid has all been absorbed, in an open saucepan.
4 Season very well before serving and a little Marsala could be added.
5 Serve with grated cheese.

Variations

Without livers – follow the above recipe but omit the chicken livers and use more mushrooms and tomatoes.

Prawn – use about 8–12 oz. prawns, adding these towards the end of stage 3, so the shellfish does not become overcooked.

Scallop – use approximately 12 scallops, put them in towards the end of stage 3.

Chicken – (a) if using uncooked chicken, cut a small frying chicken into joints and toss with the onion, mushroom and butter at stage 1.
(b) if using cooked chicken, it should be put in towards the end of stage 3.

Lingalonga peach pie

cooking time: 25 minutes

you will need for 4–6 servings:

6 oz. sweet short crust pastry, see page 72	2 egg whites
	3 oz. castor sugar
	few drops almond essence
1 lb. can sliced peaches	
2 tablespoons lemon juice	¼ pint thick cream
1 tablespoon arrowroot or cornflour	**To decorate:** glacé cherries

1 Roll out pastry and line 8-inch flan ring.
2 Bake 'blind', see page 50, until golden brown, cool.
3 Strain juice from the peaches.
4 Measure out ½ pint (if necessary make up to ½ pint with water) and add lemon juice.
5 Blend the arrowroot with 2 or 3 tablespoons of this and place remainder in a saucepan to warm.
6 Add to the blended arrowroot, return to the pan and allow the mixture to come to the boil stirring constantly.
7 Cook for 2 minutes. Add the peaches.
8 Allow to cool and pour into the baked pie case.
9 Beat the egg whites until very stiff and continue beating, gradually adding the sugar and essence.
10 Beat the cream until it will stand in soft peaks.
11 Combine the cream and whites together, folding with a tablespoon.
12 Pile this on to the pie and chill thoroughly before serving.
13 Place two or three sliced cherries on each slice to decorate.

Buffet Suppers

The following menus are for a buffet type of meal. This does not necessarily mean that your guests will not sit down to the table, but it does mean you can have the dishes arranged on the sideboard and they may help themselves.

Kedgeree

cooking time: 30 minutes

you will need for 4 servings:

8 oz. smoked haddock	2 oz. butter
6 oz. long grain rice	2 hardboiled eggs
pepper, salt and	chopped parsley
cayenne	onions, optional
1 onion	

1 Pour boiling water over the haddock, leave to stand for 5 minutes.
2 Remove any bones and skin and flake coarsely.
3 Bring a pint of salted water to boil, in large saucepan, pour in the rice, cover closely and cook over very low heat until all water is absorbed, about 25 minutes.
4 Meanwhile fry chopped onion in a little of the butter until soft and transparent. Chop whites of eggs and sieve the yolks.
5 Stir flaked fish, onion, egg whites and rest of the butter into the cooked rice and season rather highly.
6 Heat through gently and pile on flat warm dish.
7 Make a big yellow cross over the top with the sieved egg yolks and scatter whole dish with parsley.
8 For a more savoury flavour, top with fried onions.

Pizza pie

cooking time: 30–35 minutes

you will need for 4 servings:

1 lb. tomatoes	8 oz. bread dough*
pinch mixed herbs,	few slices mozzarella
oregano or marjoram	cheese
salt pepper	few black olives
small can anchovy	
fillets	

*If you do not wish to make the proper yeast dough, see right then use a scone dough, see page 60.

1 Skin the tomatoes and cook gently with the herbs and seasoning until a thick purée, stirring from time to time, so the mixture does not stick.
2 Add half the chopped anchovy fillets, put over the bread dough which should be pressed into an 8-inch greased and floured sandwich tin.
3 Allow to prove in a warm place for about 15 minutes.
4 If using the scone dough, you will not put this to prove since it contains no yeast.
5 Cook just above the centre of a hot oven (425–450°F.–Gas Mark 6–7), for approximately 15 minutes.
6 Arrange the slices of cheese and the fillets of anchovy on top and return to oven for a further 5 minutes.
7 Garnish with black olives.

Home-made bread or rolls

A home-made loaf of an interesting shape or tiny dinner rolls set the seal on a good meal. Here is a quick and easy recipe.

cooking time: 30–40 minutes

you will need:

1 lb. plain or bread	just under ½ oz. yeast
flour	1 teaspoon sugar
good teaspoon salt	approximately ½ pint
1 oz. margarine,	tepid water or milk
butter or fat	and water

1 Sieve the flour with the salt into a large bowl.
2 Rub in the butter and put into a warm place.
3 Cream the yeast with the sugar, add the tepid water.
4 Make a well in the centre of the flour mixture, put in the yeast liquid, sprinkle with a little flour and leave until the surface is covered with bubbles.
5 Knead together well until the dough is smooth.
6 You may find an appreciable amount of flour is used for kneading; on the other hand the flour may absorb a high amount of liquid and little flour is required.

7 Put the dough to prove (rise) in a warm place for a good hour.
8 Cover with a damp tea towel or polythene to keep the dough moist.
9 At the end of this time form into tiny rolls or a loaf. Put to prove once more on greased, warm baking tins or in a greased loaf tin.
10 At the end of 15 minutes, bake small rolls for approximately 12 minutes at the top of a very hot oven (475–500°F.–Gas Mark 8–9), or a loaf for approximately 20 minutes in the centre of a hot oven (425–450°F.–Gas Mark 6–7), then lower the heat to very moderate (350°F. –Gas Mark 3) for a further 20 minutes.

Variations
Milk rolls – use all milk in mixing.

Brown rolls – use $\frac{1}{2}$ wholemeal and $\frac{1}{2}$ white flour; the mixture needs to be a little softer.

Wholemeal rolls – use all wholemeal flour and make the dough really soft.

Shiny topped rolls – brush with egg before baking.

Floury topped rolls – roll the shapes into a little flour before putting to prove.

Oatmeal topped rolls – brush the top of each roll with a little milk or egg and sprinkle with rolled oats before baking.

Cheese rolls or bread – add extra seasoning and 3 oz. grated cheese to the flour.

Caramel oranges

cooking time: 5 minutes

you will need for 4 servings:

For caramel:
3 tablespoons golden syrup	6 tablespoons water
OR	
3 oz. sugar	4 firm oranges, seedless if possible

To serve:
chopped nuts	cream

1 Put the golden syrup without water, or the sugar with 3 tablespoons water, into a pan.
2 Stir until sugar has dissolved.

3 Add 3 tablespoons water to the sugar, or 6 tablespoons water to the syrup.
4 Boil steadily without stirring until a golden brown caramel.
5 Pour over the prepared oranges, which should be peeled with a sharp knife to remove all the outer pith.
6 Serve with chopped nuts and cream.

Fish cream

cooking time: 20 minutes

you will need for 16–20 hors-d'oeuvre servings:
for 6 main course servings:

2 lb. white fish*	3 tablespoons mayonnaise
1 oz. butter	
seasoning	$\frac{1}{4}$ pint thick cream
water	2 egg whites
1 level dessertspoon gelatine	

To garnish:
cucumber	mixed salad
lemon	

*Cod, hake, fresh haddock, halibut are most suitable.

1 In order to preserve the maximum flavour of the fish, wrap in buttered foil and cook for approximately 20 minutes in a moderately hot oven (400°F.–Gas Mark 5).
2 Open, pour into a measuring jug any liquid that comes from the fish during cooking.
3 Flake and pound the fish, while warm, until smooth.
4 Season very well.
5 Measure fish liquid and add enough water to give just under $\frac{1}{4}$ pint.
6 Heat and dissolve the gelatine in this, add to fish together with the mayonnaise.
7 Allow the mixture to cool and stiffen very slightly.
8 Fold in the lightly whipped cream and the stiffly beaten egg whites.
9 Taste and add extra seasoning, if needed.
10 Pour into a ring or similar mould and allow to set.
11 Turn out and garnish with cucumber and lemon or a mixed salad.

Variations

Salmon cream – use either canned or fresh cooked salmon instead of white fish.

Piquant fish cream – use a little dry sherry or wine vinegar in place of some of the water, add chopped parsley, capers and gherkins to the fish.

As a pâté – make the mixture as before (a little anchovy essence can be added to the gelatine mixture to give colour and more flavour) put into a loaf tin and cover with melted butter when set; turn out, cut in slices and serve with hot toast and butter.

Asparagus rolls and ham

no cooking

you will need for 8 servings:

8 slices ham	8 asparagus tips
little mayonnaise or soft cream cheese	

To garnish:

lemon	watercress

1 Spread the ham with mayonnaise or cream cheese.
2 Put asparagus tip on this and then roll firmly.
3 Garnish with lemon or watercress.

Variations

With salmon – use smoked salmon in place of ham.

For cornet shapes – blend chopped gherkins, parsley, or chives and capers with soft cream cheese, spread over slices of ham and roll or form into cornet shapes.

Anchovy eggs

cooking time: 10 minutes

you will need for 8 hors-d'oeuvre servings:

4 hardboiled eggs	small can anchovies

To garnish:

8 capers	watercress or mustard and cress
1 lemon, sliced	

1 Halve the eggs lengthways, remove the yolks and pound with most of the chopped anchovies and oil from the can.
2 Put back into the white cases.
3 Garnish with the rest of the anchovy fillets, capers and lemon, and serve with plenty of cress.

Pork and bacon kromeskies

cooking time: few minutes

you will need for 24 servings:

6 oz. chopped, cooked pork	12 rashers streaky bacon
6 oz. chopped, boiled bacon or ham	batter, see page 42, made with:
thick white sauce, see page 40, made with:	4 oz. flour
	1 egg
2 oz. butter	¼ pint milk and beer or all milk
2 oz. flour	seasoning
¼ pint milk	deep lard for frying
salt, pepper	
¼ teaspoon grated nutmeg	

1 Mix the pork and bacon with the sauce.
2 Season well with salt and pepper and nutmeg and spread on a plate.
3 Allow to cool.
4 De-rind the rashers and stretch each with a knife.
5 Divide each rasher in two, then place a little of the meat mixture on each and roll up.
6 Dip each kromeskie into the thick batter and fry in deep lard until golden brown.
7 Serve hot on cocktail sticks. To keep hot leave on kitchen paper, on a dish, in very low oven or on electric hot plate.

Potato and apple salad

cooking time: 20–25 minutes

you will need for 6–8 servings:

2 lb. potatoes	juice ½ lemon
8 oz. bacon	½ pint beef stock
2 eggs	salt and pepper
¼ cucumber	parsley
2 red eating apples	1 tablespoon vinegar

To garnish:
parsley

1 Peel potatoes and boil until tender.
2 Cool slightly and cut into dice, place in bowl.
3 Fry bacon until crisp and crumble into potato, reserving bacon fat.
4 Hard-boil eggs, slice cucumber.
5 Dice eating apples and dip in lemon juice.
6 Heat stock, add salt and pepper to taste, chopped parsley, vinegar and bacon fat and pour over potato.
7 Mix well, add all other ingredients, reserving some of each for garnish, with the parsley.

Cream mincemeat tarts

cooking time: 17–18 minutes

you will need for 12–16 servings:

5–6 oz. short crust or rich short crust pastry,* see page 72

approximately 12 oz. mincemeat
¼ pint thick cream
tiny pieces angelica

*Or sweet short crust pastry, see page 72.

1 Line fairly shallow patty tins with the pastry and bake 'blind' in a moderately hot oven (400°F.–Gas Mark 5) for sweet short crust pastry or a hot oven (425–450°F.–Gas Mark 6–7) for short crust, for approximately 12 minutes until golden brown.
2 Put in the mincemeat and cook for a further 5–6 minutes. Allow to cool.
3 Whip the cream, it can be sweetened if liked, and pipe round the edge of the tartlet cases, leaving just a ring of mincemeat showing.
4 Decorate with tiny pieces of angelica.

Coffee honeycomb mould

cooking time: 15 minutes

you will need for 6–8 servings:

1 large can evaporated milk
water
3 eggs
4 oz. sugar
vanilla essence

1 oz. gelatine
1 level tablespoon soluble coffee powder
6 tablespoons boiling water

To decorate:
fruit

1 Add enough water to evaporated milk to give 1½ pints.
2 Heat milk and water and pour on to egg yolks and sugar, strain and return to pan.
3 Heat, stirring until mixture thickens, taking care not to allow custard to boil, add few drops vanilla essence.
4 Dissolve the gelatine and coffee powder in the boiling water.
5 Add to the custard making sure that both mixtures are of similar temperature, then quickly fold in the stiffly whisked whites of eggs.
6 Pour into a wet 2-pint, fancy mould and leave to set.
7 Turn out and decorate with fruit.

Pineapple pork loaf

cooking time: 1½ hours

you will need for 6 servings:

1¼–1½ lb. belly pork
small can pineapple rings
2 oz. breadcrumbs
1 small onion
1 oz. fat
½ teaspoon dried or 1 teaspoon chopped, fresh sage

pinch dried thyme or 1 teaspoon chopped, fresh thyme
little grated lemon rind
1 egg
3 tablespoons milk
fat and crisp breadcrumbs for coating tin

1 Mince the pork. Put into basin and add two finely chopped pineapple rings, crumbs, finely chopped onion, fried until tender in the fat, and all the other ingredients.
2 Blend thoroughly. Grease loaf tin or small oval casserole.
3 Coat with crumbs. Put in meat mixture.
4 Cover with greased greaseproof paper or foil.
5 Bake for 1¼ hours in centre of a moderate oven (375°F.–Gas Mark 4).
6 Turn out and coat with pineapple sauce, see below.
7 Garnish with baked tomatoes and peas.

Variations

With mandarin oranges – use mandarin oranges instead of pineapple.

With tomato – use medium-sized can tomatoes instead of fruit, and only 1 tablespoon milk.

Pineapple sauce

cooking time: 10 minutes

you will need:

1 oz. margarine
1 oz. flour
syrup and fruit left from loaf

½ pint stock or water
seasoning

1 Heat the margarine in pan.
2 Stir in the flour and cook for several minutes until flour turns golden brown.
3 Add enough stock to pineapple syrup to give ½ pint.
4 Add to margarine mixture.
5 Bring to the boil, stirring until smooth.
6 Add halved or quartered rings of pineapple, plenty of seasoning and pour over loaf.

Beef darioles

cooking time: 20–25 minutes

you will need for 6 servings:

3 eggs
8 oz. sweet corn
¼ pint milk
8 oz. chopped or minced, cooked beef
salt, pepper
3 medium-sized tomatoes

1 Beat the eggs well, then add sweet corn, milk, meat and seasoning.
2 Grease dariole moulds and put half a tomato in the bottom of each dariole.
3 Pour the mixture over the tomatoes.
4 Bake for about 20–25 minutes in a moderate oven (375°F.–Gas Mark 4) until custard sets.
5 Serve at once.

Variations

Tuna fish darioles – follow above recipe replacing beef with canned tuna.
Cheese darioles – follow above recipe using grated cheese instead of beef.

Balmoral tartlets*

cooking time: 30–35 minutes

you will need for 9–12 tartlets:

8 oz. rough puff pastry, see page 65
4 oz. butter
4 oz. sugar
2 eggs
3 oz. cake crumbs
4 oz. currants

*An old-fashioned favourite, ideal to serve as a sweet, or for tea.

1 Roll out the pastry, cut rounds with a cutter a size larger than the patty pans, line pans with the rounds. Leave a little pastry over.
2 Beat butter and sugar until creamy.
3 Separate yolks from whites of eggs and beat yolks into butter and sugar, one at a time.
4 Pass cake crumbs through a fine sieve and clean currants, whisk egg whites stiffly.
5 Stir these into other ingredients and fill patty pans with mixture.
6 Roll out remaining pastry, cut into strips, twist each strip and place across patties, two on each, crossing each other.
7 Bake in a moderately hot oven (400–425°F.–Gas Mark 5–6) for about 30–35 minutes.
8 When cooked take out of tins and place on a sieve to cool. Serve with cream.

Stuffed fruits

Most fruits can be stuffed to serve as a sweet. If standing for a long time, it is better to use canned pears and peaches which do not discolour.

Stuffed peaches

Fill with whipped thick cream, with added chopped glacé cherries, chopped nuts, a little sugar to sweeten.

Stuffed pears

Fill with whipped thick cream, with added chopped crystallised ginger and chopped nuts.

Coconut stuffed fruit

Fill with rather coarsely desiccated coconut and sugar blended with whipped thick cream.

Marzipan stuffed fruits

Make, see below, or buy marzipan, and soften it a little by adding extra egg or a little sherry or brandy. Put into half peaches or pears and bake for a short time in the oven. Serve hot or cold.

To make marzipan

you will need:

8 oz. ground almonds
4 oz. castor sugar
4 oz. icing sugar
few drops almond essence
1½ egg yolks, to mix

1 Mix all ingredients together, adding enough egg yolk to make a firm mixture.
2 Knead thoroughly, do not overhandle.

Curried egg pie

cooking time: 1 hour 10 minutes

you will need for 4 servings:

6 hardboiled eggs
1 onion
1 medium-sized apple
1 oz. fat
2 tablespoons plain flour
1 tablespoon curry powder
¼ pint plus 3 tablespoons water
juice 1 lemon
1 tablespoon tomato purée
OR
2 ripe tomatoes
seasoning

8 oz. short crust pastry, see page 72
egg or milk to glaze

1 Peel and halve eggs, peel and chop onion and apple.

2 Melt fat, add onion and fry until pale gold.
3 Stir in flour and curry powder and cook until it bubbles.
4 Add water and stir until smooth.
5 Add remaining ingredients, except eggs, cover and simmer for 30 minutes, allow to cool.
6 Make pastry, roll out half, and line a 10-inch pie plate.
7 Place halved eggs, cut side down, on pastry to within 1 inch of edge.
8 Spread cold curry sauce over and between eggs.
9 Moisten pastry edge with water.
10 Roll out rest of pastry and cover pie, pressing edges well together to seal.
11 Knock up with back of knife, then press into flutes.
12 Brush top with beaten egg or milk and decorate with leaves cut from trimmings.
13 Bake towards top of hot oven (425°F.–Gas Mark 6) for 25–30 minutes.

Variation

Curried egg cobbler – prepare the curry sauce, using a little extra liquid to give a slightly thinner sauce. Arrange in a pie dish with either whole or halved hardboiled eggs. Cover with rounds of scone mixture, see page 60, and bake for approximately 15 minutes towards the top of a hot oven (425–450°F.–Gas Mark 6–7).

Pavlova pyramid

cooking time: 2½–3½ hours

you will need for 8 servings:

4 egg whites	1 teaspoon vinegar
8–10 oz. sugar	1 level teaspoon cornflour

To decorate:

canned or fresh fruit	½ pint whipped thick cream

1 Place a piece of buttered paper on a flat oven tray.
2 Beat the egg whites until very stiff.
3 Gradually add half the sugar, beating well all the time.
4 Fold in the remainder with the vinegar and cornflour, this gives a firmer meringue.
5 Tip on to buttered or oiled paper and form mixture into a perfect round, about 8 inches in diameter, and pile up in the centre.

6 Bake for 2½–3½ hours in a cool oven (225–250°F.–Gas Mark 0–½).
7 Lift on to a flat serving dish.
8 Cover pyramid with fruit and whipped thick cream.
9 If liked, stir 2 teaspoons of rum or any suitable liqueur into whipped cream.

Almond horseshoes

cooking time: 15–20 minutes

you will need for 8 crescents:

For pastry:

6 oz. plain flour	1 oz. castor sugar
3 oz. butter or margarine	1 egg
	apricot jam

For almond filling:

3 oz. ground almonds	few drops vanilla essence
1 oz. castor sugar	
1 oz. sieved icing sugar	2 drops almond essence
2 level tablespoons condensed milk	2 drops lemon juice or lemon essence

For decoration:

1 level teaspoon instant coffee	cold water to mix
4 oz. sieved icing sugar	split almonds

1 Sieve flour and rub in butter until mixture resembles breadcrumbs.
2 Mix in sugar and add sufficient beaten egg to make a stiff dough.
3 Roll out into an oblong approximately 6 × 12 inches.
4 Brush with apricot jam and cut in half lengthwise.
5 For the filling, sieve almonds and sugar together, add condensed milk and flavourings.
6 Mix with a wooden spoon then press together with the hands into a ball.
7 Roll into two long sausage shapes and place down the centre of each strip of pastry.
8 Roll up and cut into 4-inch lengths, curve into a crescent.
9 Bake on a flat tray in a moderately hot oven (400°F.–Gas Mark 5) for approximately 15–20 minutes.
10 Cool on wire tray.
11 Sieve the coffee powder and sugar, stir in the water a little at a time until the icing just finds its own level.
12 Spread a little over the top of each crescent and sprinkle over the split almonds.

Scone dough

you will need:

8 oz. flour (with plain flour 2 teaspoons baking powder)

good pinch salt
2 oz. margarine
milk to mix

1 Sieve the dry ingredients.
2 Rub in the fat, add enough milk to give a soft rolling consistency.
3 Roll to ½-inch thickness.
4 Cut into rounds and bake as Curried egg cobbler, page 59.

Gâteau supreme

cooking time: as sponge

you will need for 6–8 servings:

2–8-inch sponge rounds*

10 meringue shells, see page 24
8 blanched almonds

8 angelica leaves
1 glacé cherry

For coffee butter cream:

2 level teaspoons instant coffee

4 oz. icing sugar
2 oz. butter

For coffee glacé icing:

1 level teaspoon instant coffee
*Or use bought sponge.

4 oz. icing sugar
cold water

1 Cut sponge rounds across in halves and sandwich all four with some of the coffee butter cream.
2 Ice the top layer of sponge with the coffee glacé icing, made by sieving the instant coffee and sugar and stirring in the water, a little at a time, until the icing just finds its own level.
3 Spread a little butter cream, made by beating all ingredients together until light and creamy, or any icing left over, on each underside of meringues and press them at equal intervals round the sides of the sandwiched sponges.
4 Pipe across the top and between each meringue with the butter cream to decorate.
5 Finish with a flower shape of the almonds, forming outer petals, then leaves of angelica, then a cherry.

To make a sponge

Method 1

you will need:

3 eggs
4 oz. sugar

3 oz. flour (with plain flour use ½ teaspoon baking powder)

1 Whisk eggs and sugar until thick and fluffy.
2 Fold in the flour.
3 Put into two 8-inch greased and floured sandwich tins and bake in a moderately hot to hot oven (400–425°F.–Gas Mark 5–6) for approximately 12 minutes.

Method 2 (Victoria sandwich)

you will need:

6 oz. margarine
6 oz. castor sugar
3 large eggs

6 oz. flour (with plain flour use 1½ teaspoons baking powder)

1 Cream margarine and sugar until very soft and light.
2 Gradually beat in the eggs, stir in the flour, add a little water if the mixture seems stiff.
3 Put into two 8-inch greased and floured sandwich tins and bake for approximately 20 minutes 375°F.–Gas Mark 4.

Salmon mousse

cooking time: 10 minutes

you will need for 6 hors-d'oeuvre servings: for 3 main course servings:

1 oz. butter
1 tablespoon finely chopped onion
1 oz. flour
½ pint milk
pinch thyme, bay leaf, little grated nutmeg
8 oz. salmon, either canned, or cooked fresh salmon
1 level dessertspoon gelatine

2 oz. stoned, chopped black olives
2 sticks celery, diced
1 lb. red eating apples
2 tablespoons tomato ketchup
3 tablespoons mayonnaise, see page 44
salt and pepper
juice 1 lemon

To garnish:

black olives
watercress

¼ cucumber

1 Melt butter in a saucepan, and gently fry the onion until transparent but not brown.
2 Stir in the flour and cook gently for 3 minutes.
3 Add milk gradually, stirring all the time.
4 Add thyme, bay leaf and nutmeg, and simmer over a low heat for 10 minutes.
5 Remove bay leaf and cool sauce.
6 Flake salmon finely and beat into sauce.
7 Add gelatine which has been dissolved in 2 tablespoons water, chopped olives, celery and 1 diced raw eating apple.

8 Stir in tomato ketchup and mayonnaise, season to taste with salt and pepper.
9 Pile into a serving dish and chill.
10 Just before serving, garnish with rest of apples, cut into slices and dipped in lemon juice.
11 Fill the centre of the dish with more black olives, cucumber, finely sliced, and watercress.

Variations

Simple salmon mousse – use the recipe as above, but omit the apple and the tomato ketchup.

Fish mousse – use either of the salmon mousse recipes, but use flaked white fish instead. Add 2 or 3 drops anchovy essence for extra flavour.

Cole slaw

no cooking

you will need for 4–6 servings:

1 small Savoy or firm white cabbage	salt, pepper
2 dessertspoons olive oil	1–2 tablespoons mayonnaise, see page 44
1 dessertspoon vinegar	

1 Shred the cabbage finely.
2 Mix all the other ingredients in a bowl.
3 Pour over the cabbage and toss.
4 Stand a little before using.

Variations

Fruit cole slaw – add finely chopped dessert apples and sultanas to the cabbage.

Golden cole slaw – use rather less cabbage, and 2–3 large grated raw carrots.

Crispy cole slaw – do not prepare the cabbage too early; add finely diced celery, apple, and a few chopped nuts.

Piquant cole slaw – add diced cucumber or gherkins, chopped pickled onions and/or walnuts and capers.

Bacon salad

no cooking

you will need for 4–6 servings:

8–12 oz. cooked bacon	1 tablespoon tomato sauce
8 oz. cooked new potatoes	dash tabasco sauce
chopped mint	dash lemon juice
chopped parsley	salt and pepper
4 tablespoons mayonnaise	shredded lettuce
	radishes
	cucumber

1 Dice bacon and potatoes and toss with the mint and parsley.
2 Blend the mayonnaise, sauces and lemon juice together in a basin, season well.
3 Add the bacon mixture and fold in carefully.
4 Pile this mixture on to shredded lettuce.
5 Garnish with radishes and cucumber.

Variation

Chef's salad – dice 4 oz. cooked tongue, 4 oz. cooked chicken, 4 oz. cooked bacon or ham and use in place of cooked bacon in the salad above. Instead of 8 oz. cooked potatoes, use 4 oz. cooked potatoes, 4 oz. cooked carrots and a little finely chopped raw celery.

Golden rice salad

cooking time: 25 minutes

you will need for 4–6 servings:

4 oz. long grain rice	1 teaspoon made mustard
$\frac{1}{2}$ pint chicken stock or water	2–3 oz. finely diced celery
$\frac{1}{2}$ teaspoon salt	3 chopped hardboiled eggs
1 small onion	2–3 tablespoons mayonnaise
2 tablespoons olive oil	
1 tablespoon white vinegar	
pepper	

To garnish:

lettuce	hardboiled egg
little chopped ham or bacon	

1 Place the rice, stock, salt and chopped onion in a large pan with a well-fitting lid.
2 Bring to the boil, stirring once or twice.
3 Reduce the heat, cover the pan and simmer for about 15 minutes, until cooked.
4 Blend together the olive oil, vinegar, pepper and made mustard, pour on to the hot rice and mix well.
5 Set aside to cool.
6 Add remaining ingredients to the rice, toss lightly and chill thoroughly.
7 Serve on lettuce leaves with cooked, diced bacon and garnish with sliced hardboiled egg.
8 Serve with cold chicken, turkey or ham, which can be sliced or cut into neat joints.

Russian salad

no cooking

you will need for 4–6 servings:

8 oz. cooked potatoes	4 oz. cooked turnip*
8 oz. cooked carrots*	2 tablespoons oil
8 oz. cooked peas*	1 tablespoon vinegar
8 oz. cooked runner	seasoning
or French beans*	

To serve:

lettuce	mayonnaise, see page 44

*Or use cooked mixed frozen vegetables.

1 Cut the vegetables into neat dice.
2 Put into a large bowl and pour over oil and vinegar, season well.
3 Leave for several hours, turning round in the dressing from time to time.
4 Do this gently so the vegetables are not broken.
5 To serve, pile on lettuce, form into a pyramid, and pour over just enough mayonnaise to coat.

Variations

Piquant salad – add diced gherkins, capers and chopped chives, spring onions or a little grated onion.

Crispy Russian salad – add diced celery and dessert apple to the vegetables before tossing in dressing.

Potato salad

cooking time: 25 minutes

you will need for 4–6 servings:

1 lb. potatoes	good pinch each salt, pepper, mustard
3 tablespoons olive oil	
2 tablespoons white malt or wine vinegar	2 teaspoons chopped parsley
1 tablespoon white wine	2 teaspoons chopped chives
	lettuce

1 Boil potatoes. If using new potatoes, boil in skins, then rub off skin.
2 While still warm, dice and mix with all ingredients, except lettuce.
3 Serve very cold on bed of lettuce.

Peach and strawberry delight

cooking time: few minutes

you will need for 6 servings:

1 oz. cornflour	3 tablespoons hot water
2 eggs	
3 oz. castor sugar	1 large can sliced peaches
1 pint milk	
1 teaspoon vanilla essence	12 oz.–1 lb. fresh strawberries
½ oz. gelatine	

1 Mix the cornflour, egg yolks and 2 oz. sugar smoothly with a little of the cold milk.
2 Put the rest on to heat.
3 Add the mixed cornflour, stir till boiling and boil 3 minutes stirring all the time.
4 Remove from the heat and stir in the vanilla essence and the gelatine dissolved in the hot water.
5 Leave to cool.
6 Drain the peaches and chop them, reserving a few for decorating.
7 Add to the cooked mixture when it has begun to thicken.
8 Beat the egg whites stiffly, beat in the remaining sugar and fold lightly into the cornflour mixture.
9 Pour into a 2-pint ring mould and leave to set.
10 Turn out the mould, fill the centre with some of the strawberries and arrange remaining sliced peaches and strawberries around the edge.

Apple cake

cooking time: 15 minutes

you will need for 6–8 servings:

For sponge:

4 oz. flour	1½ oz. butter
4 eggs	vanilla essence
4 oz. castor sugar	

For sauce and garnish:

½ pint water	juice 1 lemon
4 oz. sugar	1 egg white
1 lb. cooking apples	2 red eating apples
rum to taste	angelica

1 Sieve flour.
2 Whisk eggs and sugar together, until light and creamy, over a bowl of hot water.
3 This should be very thick and able to stand on its own weight.

4 Fold in flour and melted butter.
5 Add few drops vanilla essence.
6 Pour into two sandwich tins and bake in a moderately hot oven (400°F.–Gas Mark 5) until well risen and golden.
7 Turn out and cool.
8 Make a syrup with water and sugar and boil for 2 minutes.
9 Add peeled, cored and sliced apples and cook to a purée.
10 Put through a sieve and cool.
11 Stir in rum to taste and lemon juice.
12 Whisk white of egg stiffly and fold in.
13 Place some of this sauce between the layers of sponge, sandwich together and coat the top and sides with the rest of the sauce.
14 Decorate with slices of red eating apple, dipped in lemon juice, and angelica.

Drinks for supper parties

On page 87 you will find a brief description of your choice of wines for dinner or supper, but the following drinks are suitable for both parties. They are not only interesting, but they do make wines go a little further.

Cider cup

cooking time: 10 minutes

you will need for 10–12 glasses:

3 oz. sugar
¼ pint water
rind and juice
  2 lemons
rind and juice
  2 oranges

2 pints cider*
ice cubes
little soda water

To garnish:

cucumber slices
sprigs borage or mint

apple slices
orange slices

*Most cider is alcoholic, but it is possible to obtain non-alcoholic if you wish.

1 Boil the sugar and water with the fruit rinds.
2 Strain over the fresh fruit juices, then add the cider.
3 Pour into a bowl over ice cubes.
4 Just before serving add soda water.
5 Decorate with the slices of cucumber, sprigs of borage or mint and the sliced apple and orange.

Variations

White wine cup – use a sweet Sauternes in place of cider.

Claret cup – use Claret in place of cider and increase the amount of lemons to three and decrease the oranges to one.

Vin rosé cup – vin rosé makes a most attractive looking cup. Use in place of cider, but omit the orange juice and rind since it spoils the colour.

Cold Hallowe'en punch

no cooking

you will need for about 18 glasses:

2 bottles white wine
1 liqueur glass brandy
  or rum

¼ pint fresh orange
  juice
¼ pint bottled apple
  juice

To decorate:

crushed ice

rings of lemon and
  apple

1 Mix all the ingredients together.
2 Pour over crushed ice and serve in attractive bowls or glasses decorated with the fruit.
3 Other diced fruit, such as canned pineapple, could be added if wished.

Variation

With tea – in place of apple juice, use ¼ pint of very well strained China or Indian tea.

Sleigh ride cider cup

cooking time: 10 minutes

you will need for 8 glasses:

1 quart dry cider
2 oz. sugar
12 cloves

6 inches cinnamon
  stick

1 Mix all the ingredients together and gradually bring to boiling point.
2 Remove from heat and leave to stand for 2–3 hours.
3 Strain off spices and bring to boiling point again before serving.

Variation

With white wine – really dry white wine can be used in place of cider, and the number of cloves decreased to four.

Mulled ale

cooking time: 10 minutes

you will need for 8–9 glasses:
2 pints good ale
1 glass rum or brandy
1 tablespoon sugar
pinch ground cloves
pinch powdered ginger

1 Heat all the ingredients together.
2 Serve in hot glasses or in a hot bowl.

Variation
Mulled claret – use a reasonably priced claret instead of the ale; 1 bottle is rather less than 2 pints so be sparing with the sugar.

Teenage Supper Parties

Choosing the food

Teenagers are at an age when they are generally fairly hungry people, and they do need reasonably substantial food. Because, on the whole, they dislike being organized, it is better to choose the kind of food that will not spoil if it is left for some little time. There is no need to have very expensive food; it should be interesting, have eye-appeal, but be easy to eat and serve.

Quite a number of recipes in this chapter – even some of the hot ones – can be made and transported, for very often, young people like to have a combined party where various friends all prepare part of a dish or a complete dish.

The dishes in this chapter enable the teenagers to help themselves in between dancing and listening to records, and to eat the food in the informal way that most of them prefer.

Sausage rolls

cooking time: 20 minutes

you will need for 12 rolls:
8 oz. flaky pastry
For filling:
1 lb. sausages or
   sausage meat
little flour
little beaten egg

1 Make pastry.
2 Dip sausages in cold water, slit skins and remove them.
3 Flour the sausages or sausage meat and make into two rolls about 14 inches long.
4 Roll out pastry into a thin strip, trim off edges and divide in half lengthways.
5 Brush edges with egg, put a roll of sausage on each strip.
6 Roll up and press securely at the edge.
7 Cut each roll into six with a sharp knife, mark twice across the top with the back of the knife.
8 Brush with egg and place on an ungreased baking sheet in centre of a hot oven (450°F.– Gas Mark 7) for 20 minutes.

Flaky pastry

cooking time: as individual recipe
you will need:
8 oz. flour
pinch salt
5–6 oz. fat
water to mix

1 Sieve flour with salt.
2 Divide fat into three portions and rub one portion into flour.
3 Mix to a rolling consistency with cold water and roll out to oblong shape.
4 Cut second portion of fat into small pieces and lay on two thirds of the dough, leaving remaining third without fat.
5 Fold two of the corners over second third to make an 'envelope' with its flap open.
6 Fold over top end of pastry so closing the envelope.
7 Turn pastry at right angles and seal open ends.
8 'Rib' at intervals with a rolling pin to give a corrugated effect, thus equalising the pressure of air and so making certain the pastry will rise evenly.
9 Repeat the process using the remaining fat and turning pastry in same way.
10 Roll out once more and put into a cold place for 30 minutes if it feels very soft and sticky.
11 Fold pastry as before, turn, seal edges and 'rib' again.

12 Altogether the pastry should have three foldings and three rollings.
13 Stand in a cold place for a little while, before baking, to make the pastry rise better.
14 Cooking temperatures and times are given in individual recipes, but as a general rule bake in a very hot oven (475°F.–Gas Mark 8) for the first 15 minutes, then lower the heat to Gas Mark 5–6, or turn an electric oven off to finish cooking.

Rough puff pastry

This is made with equal quantities of fat and flour. The fat should be cut roughly into the flour sieved with salt, the dough mixed with cold water or water and a squeeze of lemon juice, then rolled out into an oblong, folded, rolled as flaky pastry above, but giving five foldings, five rollings, before using. Then use as recipes.

Surprise snacks

cooking time: 12 minutes

you will need for 12–16 servings:

8 oz. plain flour	2 oz. finely grated
1 level teaspoon salt	Cheddar cheese
1 level teaspoon dry	1 egg yolk mixed with
mustard	2 tablespoons cold
shake pepper	water
4 oz. butter or	egg white for brushing
margarine	

Fillings are varied to taste. Choose two or three or more of such titbits as stuffed olives, stoned green and black olives, chopped gherkins, chopped hardboiled egg, rolled anchovies, teaspoonsful of cottage cheese with chives, small pieces sardines, shrimps or prawns, slices cocktail sausage, cocktail onions, small cubes Dutch, Cheddar or blue cheese, small cubes cooked meat.

1 Sift flour, salt, mustard and pepper into bowl.
2 Rub in butter. Add cheese, then mix to a very stiff paste with the egg yolk and water.
3 Turn out onto a lightly floured board, knead quickly till smooth.
4 Roll out thinly and cut into 2½-inch squares.
5 Put any of the fillings into centre of each square, moisten edges of pastry with water and fold over to form triangles.
6 Press edges firmly together to seal.
7 Transfer to greased baking trays and brush with lightly beaten egg white.

8 Bake towards top of a hot oven (425–450°F.–Gas Mark 6–7) for 12 minutes.
9 Serve hot or cold.

Crusty French wedges

no cooking

you will need for 6–8 servings:

2 French loaves	1 cucumber
butter	12 small firm tomatoes
12 cheese slices	1 lettuce
1 small jar sweet	pepper, salt
pickles	mustard
2 jars chicken and	
ham paste	

1 Slice bread down in ½-inch slices, but not quite through the bottom crust.
2 Spread facing slices, in pairs, with butter and slip a slice of cheese in between every other pair, adding pickle.
3 Spread alternate pairs with savoury paste, adding a slice or two of cucumber.
4 Pack bread in polythene or foil.
5 Pack also tomatoes, lettuce and seasonings.

Sugar plum ring

cooking time: 20–25 minutes

you will need for 6–8 servings:

8 oz. self-raising flour	½ oz. castor sugar
large pinch salt	about ¼ pint cold milk
2 oz. butter	to mix

For coating:

2 oz. melted butter	few blanched
2 oz. castor sugar	almonds, seeded
mixed with	raisins and halved
1 heaped teaspoon	glacé cherries
cinnamon	1 tablespoon
	marmalade or
	honey

1 Sift together flour and salt.
2 Rub in butter, add sugar then mix to a soft, but not sticky, dough with the milk.
3 Form quickly into 18 balls, dip in melted fat then coat all over with the sugar and cinnamon.
4 Arrange balls (with a little space between each) in two layers in a well-greased 7–8-inch ring mould, scattering with almonds, seeded raisins and cherries in between.
5 Bake towards the top of a hot oven (425°F.–Gas Mark 6) for 20–25 minutes.
6 Remove from oven, brush top with warmed marmalade or honey and serve warm with butter or cream.

Apple meringue slices

cooking time: 40–45 minutes

you will need for 6-8 servings:
For pastry:
5 oz. plain flour   3 oz. margarine
3 oz. castor sugar   1 egg yolk

For filling:
5 large cooking apples   meringue made with
4–5 oz. sugar   2 egg whites, see
1 egg yolk   page 24

1 Sieve the flour into a bowl and add the sugar.
2 Rub the margarine into the mixture until it resembles fine breadcrumbs.
3 Bind together with the egg yolk and roll into a rectangle to fit a greased baking sheet 12×8 inches.
4 You can if you wish cut this into four strips 12×12 inches.
5 Bake in a moderate oven (375°F.–Gas Mark 4) for 10–15 minutes.
6 Peel, core and slice the apples and put them into a saucepan with the sugar.
7 Stew gently until tender, then beat in the egg yolk.
8 Spread the apple purée over the pastry.
9 Make the meringue and place into a piping bag or syringe with a ½-inch plain pipe.
10 Pipe decoratively over the apple mixture.
11 Return to oven and bake until meringue is golden brown.*
12 Cut into required slices when cold.

*The Italian meringue, see below, tends to be more suitable for this type of mixture, but either can be used. Set at a very much lower temperature, i.e. (300°F.–Gas Mark 2) for approximately 30 minutes until the top of the meringue is tipped with golden brown.

Italian meringue

you will need:
1 lb. granulated or   ¼ pint water
   castor sugar   whites of 2 large eggs

1 Put the sugar and water into a pan and stir until the sugar has thoroughly dissolved.
2 Boil steadily until the mixture reaches a fairly firm 'soft ball', 240°F.
3 Whisk the whites of the eggs until they are very stiff and gradually whisk in the sugar syrup.

4 Pipe or pile as ordinary meringue on to oiled paper and set in a cool oven, (225–250°F.–Gas Mark 0–½).

Chocolate meringue

The Italian meringue gives a particularly good chocolate result. Make as before to stage 2, then pour the syrup on to 4 oz. melted chocolate and then on to the stiffly beaten egg whites.

Walnut cheese balls

no cooking

you will need for 20 balls:
parsley   2 oz. chopped dates
8 oz. cream cheese   lettuce
2 oz. chopped walnuts

1 Chop a little parsley and add to other ingredients, except lettuce.
2 Form into twenty tiny balls.
3 Serve cold on lettuce.

Chicken and rice pompoms

cooking time: 30 minutes

you will need for 4-6 servings:
6 oz. cooked rice   12 oz. diced chicken
2 oz. celery, chopped   2 oz. melted butter
3 oz. chopped walnuts   2 eggs
3 tablespoons minced   3 oz. coarsely chopped
   onion   walnuts
½ teaspoon salt   1 teaspoon butter
⅛ teaspoon pepper

To serve:
hot chicken gravy or chicken noodle soup

1 Combine rice, celery, walnuts, onion, salt, pepper and chicken.
2 Add melted butter and beaten eggs to moisten.
3 Shape into twelve 2-inch balls.
4 Place in greased shallow pan.
5 Bake in a hot oven (425–450°F.–Gas Mark 6–7) for about 30 minutes until crisp.
6 About 10 minutes before serving put walnuts in shallow pan, dot with the butter and toast in oven, stirring once.
7 Serve chicken balls with hot chicken gravy or chicken noodle soup and garnish with the toasted walnuts.

Dundee orange tart

cooking time: 35–40 minutes

you will need for 5–6 servings:
6 oz. short crust pastry, see page 72
For filling:
3 oz. butter or margarine
3 oz. castor sugar
2 level teaspoons finely grated orange rind
1 egg
To decorate:
1½ oz. almonds, blanched and halved
3 level tablespoons black treacle
1 oz. ground almonds
4 oz. flour (with plain flour use 1 level teaspoon baking powder)
juice ½ orange, about 2 tablespoons

1 Roll out the pastry and line a 7–8-inch oven-proof pie plate.
2 Spread with black treacle.
3 Cream the fat and sugar together with the orange rind until light and fluffy.
4 Beat in the egg, stir in the ground almonds, then fold in the sieved flour alternately with the orange juice.
5 Put the mixture into the pastry case, spread evenly, then decorate with the almonds.
6 Bake in the centre of a hot oven (425–450°F.–Gas Mark 6–7) for 20 minutes, then reduce the heat to very moderate (300–350°F.–Gas Mark 2–3) for a further 15–20 minutes.
7 This is equally good cold, topped with ice cream.

Egg boats

cooking time: 10 minutes to boil eggs

you will need for 16 boats:
16 small bread rolls
4 hardboiled eggs
2 tablespoons mayonnaise
butter
4 medium-sized tomatoes

1 Cut the top off bread rolls.
2 Scoop out some of the crumbs.
3 Mix with chopped egg and mayonnaise.
4 Butter the rolls and fill with egg mixture.
5 Remove seeds from tomatoes and decorate boats with a quartered tomato pierced with a cocktail stick to represent the sail.

Variations
Salad egg boats – mix diced cucumber, radishes, celery, with the mayonnaise.
Ham egg boats – use 4 oz. finely diced ham, 2 hardboiled eggs and little extra mayonnaise.

Cheese quoits

cooking time: 3–4 minutes

you will need for 16–18 quoits:
8 oz. plain flour
½ level teaspoon salt
3 level teaspoons baking powder
pinch dry mustard
3 oz. butter
4 oz. grated cheese
1 egg
3 tablespoons milk
deep fat for frying

1 Sieve flour, salt, baking powder and mustard into a basin.
2 Rub in butter and mix in cheese.
3 Whisk egg with milk and mix into dry ingredients to give a stiff dough.
4 Roll out ½-inch thick on a lightly floured board.
5 Cut into rings, using cutters of 2½-inch and 1¼-inch diameter.
6 Fry in hot deep fat (350°F.) until golden brown on underside – turn and fry on other side, approximately 3–4 minutes altogether.
7 Drain on kitchen paper and serve hot or cold.

Banana dessert cake

cooking time: 50–60 minutes

you will need for 8 servings:
8 oz. plain flour
large pinch salt
1 level teaspoon bicarbonate soda
5 oz. butter or magarine
4 oz. castor sugar
3 large eggs
2 medium-sized bananas
1 oz. chopped walnuts
2 tablespoons milk
1 tablespoon lemon juice

To decorate:
thick cream
walnuts
custard, if served hot

1 Sift dry ingredients.
2 Cream butter and sugar till light and fluffy, then beat in eggs, one at a time, adding a tablespoon flour with each.
3 Stir in mashed bananas and nuts, then gently fold in rest of flour alternately with the milk and lemon juice.
4 Turn into a well-greased 7-inch square cake tin, lined on the bottom with greaseproof paper.
5 Bake in the centre of a moderate oven (375°F. –Gas Mark 4) for 50–60 minutes or till cake is well risen and firm.
6 Serve cold topped with whipped cream and walnuts or hot with cream or custard.

Apple gingerbread surprise

cooking time: 40–45 minutes

you will need for 6–8 servings:
For cake:

4 oz. flour (with plain
 flour use 1 teaspoon
 baking powder)
½ teaspoon salt
1½ level teaspoons
 ginger

1 level teaspoon
 grated nutmeg
4 oz. butter
4 oz. soft brown sugar
grated rind 1 lemon
juice 1 lemon
2 eggs

For topping:

2 oz. butter
2 oz. brown sugar

2 tart dessert apples
cherries, optional

1 Sift the flour, salt and spices together.
2 Cream the butter and sugar with the lemon rind and juice until light and fluffy.
3 Beat in the eggs one at a time then fold in the sieved flour.
4 For the topping, cream together the butter and sugar, spread over the bottom and sides of an 8-inch cake tin.
5 Peel, core and slice apples and arrange slices evenly over the base.
6 Spread the cake mixture carefully over the apples.
7 Bake in a moderate oven (375°F.–Gas Mark 4) for 40–45 minutes.
8 Turn out on to a dish and decorate with cherries, if liked.
9 Serve hot with cream or cold (but freshly baked) with ice cream.

Ham stuffed eggs

cooking time: 10–12 minutes

you will need for 12 servings:

6 large eggs
1 oz. butter
2 tablespoons cream
 or mayonnaise

1 slightly rounded
 teaspoon made
 mustard
4 oz. finely chopped
 ham
salt

To garnish:

paprika
parsley

sliced cocktail onions

1 Hard boil the eggs.
2 Slice each in half lengthways and turn yolks into a basin and pound well.
3 Cream butter until soft then gradually add to egg yolks, cream, mustard, ham, and salt to taste.
4 Beat till smooth, if the mixture is a little stiff add more cream or top of the milk.
5 Spoon into egg white halves and garnish.
6 Serve with crusty buttered rolls or Pepperpot nut sticks, see below.

Saturday cheeseburgers

cooking time: 15–20 minutes

you will need for 6 servings:

12 oz. topside steak
1 slice bread
1 medium-sized
 onion
good sprinkling black
 pepper
1 level teaspoon salt

1 oz. butter or bacon
 dripping
6 thin slices Cheddar
 or processed cheese
6 soft (bap) rolls
little made mustard
salad

1 Mince the steak, bread and onion.
2 Season with pepper and salt.
3 Form into six flat cakes.
4 Place in grill pan without rack.
5 Top with butter or bacon dripping.
6 Grill under medium heat, turning carefully two or three times, and allowing about 5–7 minutes each side.
7 Spoon pan drippings over the burgers.
8 Place a slice of cheese on bottom half of each roll.
9 Dab with mustard and top with hot burger.
10 Place buttered tops of rolls over.
11 Serve with crisp lettuce or cress and tomatoes or baby beetroot.

Pepperpot nut sticks

you will need:

cheese straws, see
 page 10
pepper

cayenne pepper
1 oz. chopped walnuts

1 Use the recipe for cheese straws, but add a very generous amount of pepper, including cayenne pepper, to the seasoning.
2 Blend 1 oz. chopped walnuts with the grated cheese.
3 Cut into fingers like cheese straws, serve round the Ham stuffed eggs with an easy to eat mixed salad or potato salad, see pages 52 and 62.

Brandy snaps

cooking time: 8–12 minutes each batch

you will need for 18 biscuits:

2 oz. flour	2 level tablespoons
2 oz. margarine or	golden syrup
butter or cooking fat	½ level teaspoon
2 oz. sugar	powdered ginger
	thick cream

1 Take 1 teaspoon of flour away, so scales no longer give quite 2 oz.
2 Put margarine, sugar and golden syrup into a saucepan.
3 Mix flour and ginger together.
4 Allow margarine to melt slowly, then take pan off heat and stir in flour.
5 Grease two or three baking tins very well indeed, do not flour.
6 Put teaspoons of the mixture on the trays, allowing about 3 inches all round, since they spread out a great deal.
7 As rolling takes several minutes put one tray into the oven to begin with, setting it at a very moderate heat (325–350°F.–Gas Mark 3).
8 The biscuits take 8–12 minutes to cook but you can look into the oven after 5 minutes and again a little later.
9 They are ready to remove from the oven when uniformly golden brown.
10 Put a second tin into the oven after about 5 minutes, then the third tin after about 10 minutes.
11 Keep trays as near middle of oven as possible.
12 When first tray comes out of oven don't touch the biscuits for about 2 minutes, since they are very soft.
13 Test after 2 minutes to see if you can slip a palette knife under them, if so they are ready to roll.
14 Grease the handle of a wooden spoon, lift biscuit from tray, then press round spoon.
15 Hold in position for a few seconds to give biscuit a chance to set.
16 Slip out handle of spoon and put biscuit on a wire sieve.
17 Do the same with the next biscuit, trying to work quickly with each tray, as when biscuits start to harden they cannot be removed from tin.
18 If this happens to last one or two, put tin back in oven for a minute and start testing again when you bring out the warmed biscuits.
19 Store *away from all* other biscuits, and cakes, in airtight jar or tin.
20 Fill biscuits with lightly whipped cream just before serving.

Eccles cakes

cooking time: 12–15 minutes

you will need for 15 cakes:

8 oz. flaky or puff	4 oz. currants
pastry, see pages	2 oz. mixed cut peel
64 and 70	½ level teaspoon
1 oz. margarine	mixed spice
1 level tablespoon	sugar and water to
soft brown sugar	glaze

1 Make the pastry.
2 To make the filling, melt the margarine in a saucepan and stir in the other ingredients.
3 Leave to cool.
4 Roll out the pastry thinly on a floured board, cut into rounds with a 3½-inch cutter.
5 Put one heaped teaspoon of filling in the centre of each.
6 Brush the pastry edges with water, gather the outside edges over the filling and press together at top to seal.
7 Turn the cakes over so the sealed ends are underneath, roll each with the rolling pin into round flat shapes.
8 Make three slits on each with a knife.
9 Brush with water and sprinkle with castor sugar.
10 Bake in a hot oven (450°F.–Gas Mark 7) on second shelf from top for 12–15 minutes.

Puff pastry

cooking time: as individual recipe

you will need:

8 oz. plain flour	few drops lemon juice
pinch salt	7–8 oz. butter or
cold water to mix	margarine

1 Sieve flour and salt, then mix to a rolling consistency with water and lemon juice.
2 Roll to an oblong shape.
3 Make fat into neat block and place in centre of pastry and fold over it first the bottom section of pastry and then the top section, so that the fat is quite covered.
4 Turn dough at right angles, seal edges and 'rib' carefully, roll out.
5 Fold dough into envelope, turn, seal edges, 'rib' and roll again.
6 Repeat five times, so making seven rollings and seven foldings in all.
7 Rest pastry in cold place once or twice between rollings to prevent it becoming sticky and soft.
8 Always rest it before rolling for the last time and before baking.
9 Bake in a very hot oven (475°F.–Gas Mark 8) for the first 10–15 minutes then reduce heat to moderate (375°F.–Gas Mark 4) to finish cooking.

Picburgers with salad

cooking time: 10 minutes

you will need for 8 servings:

8 soft rolls	pepper, salt
butter	8 cheese slices
1 lb. fresh minced steak	made mustard
2 dessertspoons plain flour	sweet pickle

1 Split and butter rolls.
2 Mix meat and flour and season.
3 Shape into sixteen thin, round cakes.
4 Place slice of cheese on eight, spread with made mustard and then press the remaining eight cakes on top.
5 Place in grill pan without rack.
6 Grill slowly 5 minutes each side, dabbing with butter, if the meat is very lean.
7 Allow to become quite cold.

8 Place in buttered rolls with sweet pickle.
9 Serve with potato salad, see page 62, Russian salad, see page 62, or cole slaw, see page 61.

Mexicorn tartlets

cooking time: 10 minutes

you will need for 12–18 savouries:

6 oz. short crust or cheese biscuit crust, see pages 72 and 10	½ can corn and red pepper
	4 oz. cream cheese

1 Line patty tins approximately 1–1½-inches in diameter with very thin short crust or cheese biscuit crust pastry.
2 Bake 'blind' in a hot oven (425–450°F.–Gas Mark 6–7) for approximately 10 minutes until crisp and golden brown.
3 Drain the canned corn and pepper.
4 Blend most of this with the cheese and put into the pastry cases.
5 Top with the rest of the corn, pressing this into the cheese so it will not drop off.

Chocolate mallow

cooking time: 40–45 minutes

you will need for 6 servings:

4 oz. self-raising flour	2 eggs
1 oz. cornflour	2 oz. walnuts, coarsely chopped
1 oz. cocoa	
pinch salt	4 oz. (about 20) pink and white marshmallows
4 oz. butter or margarine	
3 oz. soft brown sugar	4 tablespoons milk

1 Sift together dry ingredients.
2 Cream fat and sugar until light and fluffy, then beat in eggs one at a time.
3 Add the walnuts and 14 marshmallows, halved.
4 Fold in dry ingredients alternately with the milk and turn mixture into a well-greased 2 pint oven-proof dish.
5 Bake in the centre of a moderate oven (375°F. –Gas Mark 4) for 40–45 minutes.
6 Remove from oven, mark top into six portions and placed a halved marshmallow on each portion.
7 Return to oven for 2–3 minutes for mallows to melt slightly.
8 Serve warm, or very fresh with cream.

Menus With At Least One Hot Dish

In winter time particularly, it is a good idea to have at least one simple hot dish. As you will see from the following menus, these need not be elaborate in any way, and probably everyone will enjoy helping to cook them.

Barbecue chicken

cooking time: 30 minutes

you will need for 4 servings:
2 small frying chickens   barbecue sauce, see
melted butter   page 73

1 Brush the chickens over with melted butter.
2 If you are having an outside barbecue, they go over the charcoal on the grid; if you are cooking these on a rotisserie spit, then put the rod through the centre of the chicken, or the chickens can be cooked on an indoor barbecue.
3 They will take approximately 30 minutes to cook, and during cooking keep them well basted either with butter or with the barbecue sauce.
4 Halve before serving with the barbecue sauce.

Barbecued potatoes

cooking time: 1¼–1½ hours

you will need for 8 servings:
4 large potatoes   1 large onion
knob margarine   2 large tomatoes
seasoning   fat for frying
8 oz. belly pork, cut
    into slices

1 Bake potatoes in their jackets until just tender. Cut off tops.
2 Scoop out pulp and mash with margarine and seasoning.
3 Pile back into potato cases to make neat shape with good border round outside.
4 Cut pork into neat pieces. Fry until crisp.
5 Lift on to plate and fry the finely chopped onion and sliced, skinned tomatoes in the remaining fat until soft.
6 Put pork and vegetables in centre of potato case and return to oven to reheat.

Fresh fruit salad

cooking time: 5–10 minutes for syrup

you will need for 4 servings:
1 good-sized apple   1 dessert pear
1 or 2 bananas   any other fresh fruit
1 large orange   in season
few grapes   sugar

1 Peel and slice or dice the fruit.
2 If serving straight away, there is no need to make a syrup.
3 If preparing beforehand, then a fruit syrup will keep it moist and prevent discoloration.
4 The best and most economical way to make this is to put the rind from 1 orange and/or lemon into a saucepan with about ¼ pint water and sugar to taste.
5 Simmer gently for about 5–10 minutes and strain.
6 The juice of a fresh orange can be added, or for adults a little Kirsch can be added to the syrup or sprinkled over the fruit.
7 If wished, fresh fruits can be mixed with canned fruits, which will of course provide the syrup.

Cheese dip

cooking time: 10 minutes

you will need for 4 servings:
For sauce:
1 oz. butter   8 oz. grated Cheddar,
1 oz. flour   Gruyère, or Cheshire
½ pint milk   cheese
seasoning   little squares of bread

1 Make the white sauce, if necessary this can be made some little time beforehand, covered with a piece of damp greaseproof paper to prevent a skin forming.
2 At the last moment heat the sauce, add grated cheese, and pour into a hot dish and serve at once.
3 The squares of bread are put on to forks and dipped into the hot mixture.

Variations

Tomato cheese dip — use tomato juice in place of milk.

Harlequin cheese dip — add a little canned corn on the cob or grated carrot, finely diced green pepper or peas or chopped parsley, tiny pieces of tomato or chopped red pepper.

Piquant patties

cooking time: 15–20 minutes

you will need for 4 servings:

8 oz. finely minced rump steak	seasoning
	1 egg
2 oz. breadcrumbs	2 oz. medium oatmeal
4 teaspoons grated horseradish	1½ oz. dripping or fat flavouring, see below

1 Mix the beef, breadcrumbs and horseradish, season highly and bind with the egg.
2 Shape into round patties, roll in the oatmeal and leave for 5 minutes.
3 Fry until golden brown on both sides, allowing 15–20 minutes gentle cooking.
4 Serve with grilled mushrooms, creamed potatoes* and a watercress salad.

To add flavour

(a) **With curry** — good pinch curry powder and a dash of Worcestershire sauce.
(b) **With tomato** – ½ – 1 tablespoon concentrated tomato purée.
(c) **With onion** – little finely grated onion.

*if prefered, make potato cakes, see below.

Potato cakes

cooking time: 20–25 minutes

you will need for 4 servings:

1 lb. peeled potatoes	1 oz. flour
1 oz. margarine	very little milk or egg
salt, pepper	little fat for frying

1 Cook the potatoes steadily in boiling salted water until just firm.
2 Take care that they do not become over-soft and watery.
3 Mash well, add the margarine, seasoning, flour, and very little milk or part of an egg to give a pliable dough.
4 Form into flat round cakes and cook steadily in a little hot fat until golden brown on either side.

5 If using left-over creamed potatoes, you may have to increase the amount of flour if the mixture is very soft.
6 If using boiled potatoes, it is easier to mash them if they are warmed for a few minutes.

Bakewell tart

cooking time: 40–45 minutes

you will need for 6 servings:

6 oz. short crust pastry, see below	3 oz. ground almonds
	1½ oz. cake crumbs
3 oz. margarine	2 tablespoons milk
3 oz. castor sugar	3 tablespoons
1 egg	raspberry jam
1 oz. plain flour	little icing sugar

1 Make the pastry and roll thinly into a round large enough to line a 7-inch flan ring (on a baking tray) or a sandwich tin.
2 Cream the margarine and sugar together until very light.
3 Beat in the egg, fold in the sieved flour, the ground almonds, cake crumbs and then the milk.
4 Spread the bottom of the flan case with raspberry jam.
5 Place the filling on the top and spread over evenly with a knife.
6 Bake in the centre of a moderately hot oven (400°F.–Gas Mark 5) for 40–45 minutes.
7 Cool slightly, remove flan ring or turn out of sandwich tin, dust lightly with icing sugar.

Short crust pastry

you will need:

8 oz. plain flour	4 oz. fat (margarine,
pinch salt	butter, or ½ margarine, ½ cooking fat)

1 Sieve flour and salt.
2 Rub in fat until like fine breadcrumbs.
3 Mix with cold water to a firm rolling consistency.

Variations

Rich short crust pastry – use all butter. You can use up to 5 oz. Blend with egg yolk and water.

Sweet short crust pastry -- add 1 oz. sugar to flour. Blend with egg yolk and water.

Meat kebabs

cooking time: 10–15 minutes

you will need for 4–6 servings:

8 oz. rump or fillet steak
8 oz. lean lamb (cut from top of leg if possible) or veal
few tiny mushrooms
butter

1 Cut the meat into small cubes and thread with the mushrooms on to four or more metal skewers.
2 Brush with melted butter and cook under a hot grill until the meat is tender.
3 Serve with the barbecue sauce, see below.

The best accompaniment to meat or sausages and the barbecue sauce are jacket potatoes topped with plenty of butter and a really crisp green salad.

Variations

With sausages – instead of the meat kebabs above, serve grilled or fried sausages to dip into the sauce.

Australian kebabs – this recipe combines the sweetness of canned fruit with meat and looks as good as it tastes. Omit the lamb and use rolls of bacon instead. Thread halved well-drained canned peaches, diced steak, mushrooms, bacon rolls, then well-drained cubes of canned pineapple on to the skewers. Blend some of the peach and pineapple syrup from the cans with the melted butter; add a good pinch mixed spice, 2–3 teaspoons Worcestershire sauce and baste the kebabs with this as they cook.

Tangy barbecue sauce

no cooking

you will need for 4–6 servings:

1 clove garlic
½ small onion
1 sprig parsley
¼ pint tomato ketchup
2 tablespoons wine vinegar
2 tablespoons oil or melted butter
1 teaspoon Worcestershire sauce
ground pepper to taste

1 Mince onion, garlic and parsley and put into a large screw top jar with all the other ingredients.
2 Cover and shake vigorously until all ingredients are well blended.
3 Leave to stand for 24 hours, shaking occasionally.
4 Use as a basting sauce or increase the amount of liquid by adding ¼ pint of stock or water and use as a sauce to serve with chops.

Marshmallow plum pie

cooking time: 35–40 minutes

you will need for 4–6 servings:

8 oz. self-raising flour
3 level teaspoons mixed spice
pinch salt
4 oz. butter or margarine
4 oz. sugar
1 egg
20–30 marshmallows
1 lb. plums

1 Sift flour, spice and salt.
2 Cream butter and sugar until light.
3 Add egg and beat well.
4 Fold in sifted dry ingredients and leave in a cool place for 30 minutes.
5 Divide mixture in two and use half to line a 9-inch shallow oven-proof dish.
6 Arrange halved and stoned plums and halved marshmallows on top.
7 Roll out remaining pastry until wafer thin to cover plums.
8 Bake just below the centre of a moderate oven (375°F.–Gas Mark 4) for 35–40 minutes.
9 Serve hot with custard or cream.

Variation

Harlequin marshmallow pie – omit plums and use a small can apricot halves, small can peach halves, and a small can pear halves. Arrange the well-drained fruit in such a way that each person will have a variety of fruits and top with the marshmallows. As the fruits have all been sweetened, you may like to sprinkle them with fresh lemon juice to make a contrast to the very sweet marshmallows.

Sausages in barbecue sauce

cooking time: 1 hour 40 minutes

you will need for 3–4 servings:

fat for frying	1 teaspoon made
12 skinless pork	mustard
sausages	1 teaspoon paprika
1 medium-sized	2 tablespoons vinegar
onion	2 sliced tomatoes
1 oz. flour	salt, pepper
½ pint water	

1 Melt fat in a large frying pan, add sausages, brown fairly quickly and remove from pan.
2 Peel and slice onion, add to remaining fat, fry till golden.
3 Stir in flour and cook, stirring until, brown.
4 Gradually add water and rest of ingredients then reheat, stirring, till mixture comes to the boil and thickens.
5 Season to taste with salt and pepper.
6 Add sausages, cover pan and simmer gently about 20 minutes.
7 Serve with freshly boiled or creamed potatoes and hot green vegetables or a crisp salad.

Double decker creole

cooking time: few minutes

you will need for 4 servings:
4 slices buttered toast

For fillings – top layer:

4 slices liver sausage	1 tablespoon finely
little mustard	chopped fried onion

Bottom layer:

3 oz. finely shredded	sprinkling salt
cabbage	1 teaspoon butter
2 tablespoons vinegar	1 teaspoon brown
	sugar

To garnish:

tomato	pickled gherkin

1 Cut slices of buttered toast across in two triangles.
2 Spread four slices of liver sausage lightly with mustard, warm under grill and top with finely chopped onion.
3 For bottom layer, boil for 1 minute shredded cabbage in the vinegar, salt, butter and brown sugar. Drain.

4 Sandwich buttered toast together with fillings, press down well, cutting across again, if liked.
5 Garnish with slices of tomato and pickled gherkin, keep warm under the grill turned low.

Speedy celery bread

cooking time: 35–40 minutes

you will need:

1 egg	1 level teaspoon salt
½ pint water	3 oz. butter or
1 packet celery soup	margarine
1 lb. self-raising flour	little milk for glazing

1 Mix the egg and water together.
2 Blend in the dry soup mix and allow to stand for 10 minutes.
3 Sieve the flour and salt and rub in the butter or margarine.
4 Pour in the soup mixture and work the ingredients together.
5 Knead into a round, put on to a greased baking sheet, flatten slightly and glaze with milk.
6 Mark off eight sections and bake in a moderately hot oven (400°F.–Gas Mark 5) for 35–40 minutes.
7 Serve freshly baked, well-buttered, with salads, cheese or soup.

Stuffed apples

no cooking

you will need for 4 servings:

4 large red apples	1 oz. walnuts, chopped
2 sticks celery,	mayonnaise, see
chopped	page 44
2 oz. raisins, chopped	few blanched almonds
2 oz. stoned dates,	
chopped	

1 Cut the tops off the apples and carefully remove the core and a little of the pulp.
2 Mix together the celery, raisins, dates, walnuts and enough mayonnaise to bind.
3 Pile into the apple cases.
4 Pipe a little mayonnaise around the edge and arrange sliced spiked almonds on top.

Variations

With meat or cheese – cubes of chicken, ham or cheese may be added to the stuffing, if liked.

With cheese and bread – serve with portions of cheese, and either crispy French bread or Speedy celery bread, ice cream, and/or fresh fruit.

Bring It With You Menus

Quite often teenagers will meet at one house, but make the supper party a combined effort, with each of them making contributions. You will find a number of dishes in this chapter that are suitable for carrying.

This is some of the equipment which will help –
1 Plastic bags for salads, which should be washed, put into the bag, and tied round tightly.
2 Foil for carrying joints of chicken to fry or ready-cooked chicken. The foil not only provides a safe covering but helps to keep the food hot.
3 Vacuum flasks for hot or cold drinks – be careful that large lumps of ice are not put into a vacuum flask – crush the ice finely. Always warm the flask well before hot drinks or hot food is put in. A wide-necked flask is ideal for carrying sauces and even stews and soups.
4 Screwtop jars can be used for carrying fruit or mixed fruit salads.

Grapefruit cocktail

you will need:

canned or fresh grapefruit	maraschino or glacé cherries
canned mandarin or fresh oranges	little sugar mint

1 If using fresh grapefruit and/or oranges, remove the segments and sprinkle with sugar.
2 If using canned grapefruit and/or oranges, use a little of the syrup only.
3 Mix the grapefruit with the oranges and cherries, and put into wide-necked vacuum flasks or screwtop jars with mint sprigs to give flavour.

Spaghetti

cooking time: 15 minutes

you will need:

1½–2 oz. spaghetti per person*	salt little butter

To serve:

tomato sauce, see below	crusty rolls butter
grated cheese	salads

*This can be cooked and carried to go with the tomato sauce.

1 Cook the spaghetti in boiling, salted water until just tender.
2 Strain, then rinse with plenty of boiling water to remove the stickiness.
3 Pour into a number of wide-necked vacuum flasks, adding a little butter.
4 Take along not only the tomato sauce, but grated cheese, crusty rolls and butter, and salads, that can also be put into screwtop jars, polythene bags, or wrapped in foil.

Tomato sauce

cooking time: 15 minutes

you will need for 4–6 servings:

1 oz. fat	½ pint water
½ apple, finely chopped	1 small can tomato purée
½ onion, finely chopped	1 beef stock cube
1 rounded teaspoon cornflour	salt, pepper

1 Melt the fat and fry the apple and onion for a few minutes.
2 Blend the cornflour with the water and stir this, with the tomato purée, into the pan.
3 Add the beef stock cube, season to taste.
4 Bring sauce to the boil and cook until it thickens, carry in small vacuum flask; warm flask first.

Date tartlets

cooking time: 15 minutes

you will need for 12 tarts:
6 oz. short crust or sweet short crust pastry, see page 72
For filling:

6 oz. dates	1 oz. brown sugar
grated rind 1 lemon	1 tablespoon syrup
¼ pint water	little lemon juice
1 oz. butter or margarine	

1 Roll out the pastry and cut into rounds.
2 Fit into twelve patty tins and bake 'blind' for 15 minutes in a hot oven (425–450°F.–Gas Mark 6–7).
3 Meanwhile chop the dates and put into a saucepan with all the other ingredients.
4 Simmer fairly briskly, stirring from time to time, until a moderately thick mixture; remember it stiffens as it cools.
5 Put into pastry cases.

Sausage and bacon surprise

cooking time: 15–20 minutes

you will need for 4 servings:

1 lb. pork sausage meat	seasoning
4 small eggs	4 rashers streaky bacon
1 teaspoon mixed herbs or basil	

1 Divide the sausage meat into four. Place on a baking tin.
2 Press a wet cup into each and press the sides up to form a hollow.
3 Remove the cup and break an egg into each.
4 Sprinkle with herbs, season with salt and pepper. Cover with halved rashers.
5 Bake for 15–20 minutes in a moderately hot oven (400°F.–Gas Mark 5).
6 Serve with fried, crispy potatoes, crisp green salad and baked stuffed tomatoes.

Baked stuffed tomatoes – these are made by choosing four tomatoes. Remove and chop the pulp, season and blend with a little canned corn on the cob or baked beans and grated cheese, put into the oven for the last 10 minutes of the cooking time above.

Lemon and strawberry cream tarts

cooking time: 10–15 minutes

you will need for 4 servings:
6 oz. sweet short crust pastry, see page 72.
For filling:

1 small can scalded evaporated milk*	1 tablespoon boiling water
2 oz. castor sugar	juice and rind 1 lemon
1 dessertspoon gelatine	4 oz. small strawberries (fresh or defrosted frozen)

*Boil for 15 minutes, open carefully.

1 Roll out pastry and line tart tins.
2 Bake 'blind', see page 50, in a hot oven (425–450°F.–Gas Mark 7) for 10–15 minutes.
3 Beat the scalded milk with the sugar.
4 Melt the gelatine in the boiling water and add the lemon juice and rind.
5 Pour this into the beaten evaporated milk and beat until thick.
6 Prepare the strawberries.
7 Fill each tart when cold with the lemon cream and top each with a small strawberry.

Chocolate pear cream tarts – follow the recipe above from stage 1 to stage 3. Melt the gelatine in the boiling water, then add 2 oz. chocolate powder and blend thoroughly. Pour into the beaten evaporated milk and when cold fill each tart with this mixture and top with sliced, well-drained, canned pears.

Chocolate pear supreme

cooking time: 20–25 minutes

you will need for 4 servings:
1 Victoria sandwich, see page 60.
For filling:

¼ pint thick cream	8 ripe dessert pears

For chocolate sauce:

4 tablespoons drinking chocolate	approximately 1 tablespoon boiling water

1 Make the Victoria sandwich.
2 Sandwich together with whipped cream and chopped pears.
3 Top with halved pears.
4 Put chocolate powder into a basin or jug, add sufficient boiling water to form a thick syrup, and stir well.
5 Just before serving, pour chocolate sauce over sandwich, and serve hot or cold.

Tray Suppers

With the advent of television, many people find that instead of being seated at a table, it is preferable to have the meal on a tray, so the favourite programme can be watched.

There are certain points to remember when you serve tray suppers, and suggestions for making these a comfortable, easy to eat and appetising meal are given below.

1 Arrange cutlery, tumblers, individual salt and pepper if possible on trays. Try to keep everything small and neat, so that a sudden movement cannot cause an accident.
2 Many of the menus in this book are suitable, but make sure cuts of meat and joints of chicken are chosen with their bones removed for it is extremely difficult to try and cut away at a bone with a tray on your lap.
3 Ideally food that can be eaten with a fork is most suitable for a tray supper.
4 To facilitate serving, have a trolley or small table at the back of the room where dishes can be put temporarily and have the next course ready, unless it must be kept warm on a hot plate or in a low oven.

You may just wish to serve a selection of toasted snacks. To save a last minute preparation, cut the slices of bread, prepare the fillings, put them in covered bowls or in foil, and then put together at the last minute.

To serve hot on toast

Fish

Kipper cheese spread

Mix equal quantities of grated cheese and flaked, cooked kipper together. Spread on hot toast, put under grill for a few minutes and garnish with pats of parsley butter.

Devilled sardines

Cream 2 oz. butter, add pinch curry powder, mustard, few drops Worcestershire sauce and spread over two–three slices of toast; arrange sardines on the toast, then sprinkle crisp breadcrumbs over sardines and heat under grill.

Escallop brochettes

Roll rashers of bacon round escallops and grill steadily. Serve on rounds of hot toast.

Prawn and grapefruit slices

Arrange peeled prawns and sections of fresh grapefruit on hot buttered toast. Brush with melted butter and heat for a few minutes.

Crispy herring roes

Coat herring roes with a little beaten egg white, crisp breadcrumbs and grated cheese. Fry until golden brown. Serve on hot toast. Garnish with paprika or cayenne pepper and parsley.

Meat

Creamed spread

Blend finely diced ham and/or chicken with a really thick white sauce, spread on the hot toast, put under the grill for a few minutes.

Ham and cheese

Put slices of ham on hot buttered toast, spread very lightly with mustard or chutney, cover with a slice of cheese and put under the grill.

Corned beef and chutney

Mix diced corned beef with a little butter and chutney, put on hot buttered toast, brush with melted butter and heat for a few minutes under the grill.

Cheese

Cheese and tomato slices

Cover hot buttered toast with slices of Cheddar cheese, top with sliced tomatoes, heat for a few minutes under the grill.

Welsh rarebit

cooking time: 12 minutes

you will need for 8 small servings:

1 oz. butter	8 oz. Cheddar cheese
1 oz. flour	1 tablespoon beer or
¼ pint milk	ale
1 teaspoon made mustard	buttered toast
salt, pepper	

1 Heat the butter in a saucepan, stir in the flour and cook steadily for several minutes, then gradually add the cold milk.
2 Bring to the boil and cook until smooth and thick.
3 Add the mustard, salt and pepper, most of the cheese, and the beer.
4 Heat steadily, without boiling too quickly, until the cheese has melted.
5 Spread over the hot buttered toast, sprinkle with the remaining cheese and brown under a hot grill.

Variations

Corn rarebit – add canned well-drained corn to the rarebit mixture.

York rarebit – put the Welsh rarebit mixture on slices of ham over hot buttered toast.

Sweet

Marshmallow fingers

Cover hot toast with a little apricot jam, then arrange pink and white marshmallows on top. Put for one minute under the grill so the marshmallows soften slightly.

Banana crispies

Cover hot buttered toast with sliced bananas. Sprinkle with brown sugar and put for one or two minutes under the grill to crisp.

Pineapple croûtes

Toast rounds of stale cake or plain buns, spread with pineapple jam, arrange rings of pineapple on top, brush with melted butter and heat under grill. Decorate with glacé cherries and glaze with more pineapple jam.

Normandy toasts

Mix chopped dates or sultanas with very thick hot apple pulp. Serve on toasted sponge cakes and top with chopped almonds.

One Dish Supper Parties

Very often the housewife is short of time, cooking facilities or space, yet wishes to provide a special dish for her guests. There are many dishes that can be served in one large container – they look gay and colourful and entail the minimum of clearing up afterwards.

The following dishes are particularly suitable:

Meat dishes

Veal blanquette	page 26
Veal roll	page 29
Veal goulash	page 84
Chinese lamb stew	page 18
Burgundy beef in red wine	page 83
Paprika pork casserole	page 21
Casserole of liver and apples	page 49
Sweetbread vol-au-vent	page 35
Cheese and ham loaf	page 84
Bacon crumb pie	page 47

Poultry dishes

Chicken cacciatore	page 28
Braised duck and cherries	page 32
Chicken with walnuts	page 51
Risotto	page 53
Avocado and chicken salad	page 86

Fish dishes

Salmon mayonnaise	page 43
Fried prawns	page 42
Haddock casserole	page 48
Fish mornay flan	page 46
Kedgeree	page 54

Savoury dishes

Spaghetti and tomato and red pepper sauce	page 52
Savoury omelettes	page 92

When the Family Takes Over

It may well be that the children or man of the house have invited guests when the mother or wife is not available to prepare the meal, and this chapter has been designed to provide gay and interesting dishes which need little, if any, cooking skill.

Expert male cooks can miss this section and use the rest of the book!

Grapefruit and shrimp cocktail

no cooking

you will need for 4 servings:

1 can grapefruit segments OR	1 small can shrimps mayonnaise
2 fresh grapefruit	

1 Mix grapefruit segments and shrimps together.
2 Use sufficient of the mayonnaise to bind.
3 Put into individual glasses or into grapefruit halves, if using fresh fruit.
4 Serve chilled.

Bacon and mushroom shells

cooking time: 10 minutes

you will need for 4 servings:

1–1½ lb. creamy mashed potatoes little egg	1 can condensed mushroom soup seasoning
12 oz. diced cooked gammon OR boiled ham	

1 Pipe the potato in a decorative border round the edges of four scallop shells, or individual dishes.
2 Brush well with little beaten egg and brown under the grill.
3 Fry the gammon in pan until warm, then add the soup and heat together. Season.
4 Pour into the centre of the shells.

Jelly delight

no cooking

you will need for 4–6 servings:

1 packet orange jelly	4 teaspoons bramble jelly
½ pint yoghourt	2 bananas

1 Make the jelly, using only ¾ pint water so that it is firmer than usual.
2 Allow to set in a refrigerator.
3 Turn out and chop into rough pieces with a very sharp knife.
4 Pile into individual dishes.
5 Spoon yoghourt on top, decorate each with a teaspoon bramble jelly, and surround with finely sliced bananas.

Baked Hawaiian gammon

cooking time: 20 minutes

you will need for 4 servings:

4 × 1-inch slices gammon*	8 cloves corn oil
1 small can pineapple slices	

To garnish:

tomato rings olives	parsley

For sauce:

1 level teaspoon dry mustard	1 level teaspoon cornflour

*You may find it looks more attractive to buy 2 very large slices gammon and divide before serving.

1 Trim the rind from the gammon and arrange slices pineapple on top of each piece.
2 Spike the gammon fat with cloves, brush with corn oil then place in an ovenproof dish.
3 Pour over pineapple juice from can, then bake for 20 minutes in a moderately hot oven (400°F.–Gas Mark 5).
4 When cooked, remove cloves and put gammon and pineapple on serving dish.
5 Garnish with tomato rings, olives and parsley.
6 Mix mustard and cornflour to a paste with one tablespoon water and add to juices from the oven dish.
7 Cook for 3 minutes on top of stove, season if liked, and serve as an accompanying sauce.

Variation

Honey peach gammon – top each slice gammon with 1 or 2 peach halves instead of pineapple slices. Continue as stage 2, but blend 1 tablespoon lemon juice and 1 tablespoon honey with the peach juice from the can at stage 3: complete the recipe as above.

Pear and grape salad

no cooking

you need for 4 servings:

2 dessert pears*
¼ pint thick cream
1 dessertspoon castor sugar
few drops vanilla essence
8 oz. grapes

*Or four canned, halved pears.

1 Peel the pears just before serving. Halve.
2 Whip the cream and sugar, add vanilla essence.
3 Halve grapes and remove the seeds.
4 Place pears on plates with the cut side down.
5 Spread each half with cream and cover with the grape halves to represent bunch of grapes.

Savoury chops

cooking time: 15 minutes

you will need for 4 servings:

4 lamb chops
1 egg
breadcrumbs
butter or oil for frying
½ cucumber
2 large tomatoes
2 oz. butter
salt, pepper

1 Dip chops in beaten egg and breadcrumbs.
2 Fry in hot butter or oil.
3 Arrange on hot dish.
4 While chops are cooking, peel cucumber and dice.
5 Skin and slice tomatoes.
6 Heat the butter in a frying pan and add cucumber, tomatoes, salt and pepper.
7 Cover closely and cook gently for 5–10 minutes or until pieces are tender.
8 Put round chops.

Coffee macaroon blancmange with chocolate sauce

cooking time: 15 minutes

you will need for 6 servings:

2 level tablespoons cornflour
2 tablespoons icing sugar
2 level tablespoons instant coffee
1 pint milk
2 large almond macaroons

For sauce:

½ pint milk
4 oz. grated chocolate
1 oz. butter
2 oz. sugar
1 teaspoon cornflour
1 tablespoon rum, optional

To decorate:

whipped thick cream
1 tablespoon finely chopped walnuts
few halved walnuts

1 Mix the cornflour, sugar and coffee smoothly with a little of the milk, heat the rest and add gradually to the cornflour mixture, stirring all the while.
2 Return to the pan and cook well, stirring until smooth and very thick.
3 Cool and stir in crushed macaroons.
4 Pour into a wetted mould and leave in a cold place to set.
5 Warm the milk for the sauce, add the grated chocolate, butter, sugar, and cornflour.
6 Cook, stirring all the time, until the sauce is thick and smooth.
7 Stir in the rum if this is to be included. Turn out mould.
8 Decorate with whipped cream or little cold sauce scattered with the chopped nuts.
9 Arrange cream and halved walnuts round it.
10 Serve the rest of the sauce separately, this could be hot if wished.

Pork and melon platter

no cooking

you will need for 4 servings:

8 slices cold roast pork
½ melon
little ground ginger
1 tomato
salad

1 Arrange the pork on a large round plate.
2 Cut melon into ½-inch slices.
3 Dust with the ginger.
4 Arrange these alternating with each slice of pork.
5 Put a tomato in the centre.
6 Serve with salad and potatoes Lyonnaise, see page 81.

Potatoes boulangère

cooking time: 2 hours

you will need for 4 servings:

4 medium-sized potatoes	seasoning
2 medium-sized onions	1 pint stock or stock and water
	1 oz. fat

1 Brush all round a 1½-pint ovenware dish with melted fat.
2 Place the peeled and sliced potatoes and onions in alternate layers in the dish, ending with a layer of potatoes.
3 Season each layer.
4 Pour in the stock, or stock and water.
5 Place small knobs of fat on the top layer of potatoes.
6 Cover with foil.
7 Place in a very moderate oven (350°F.–Gas Mark 3) on the bottom shelf in a gas oven, in the centre of an electric oven – leave for 2 hours.

Variations

Potatoes Lyonnaise – omit stock, just put plenty of thinly sliced onions and seasoning between potatoes.

Potatoes Portuguese – omit stock, put layers tomatoes and onions between potatoes.

Swiss russe

no cooking

you will need for 4 servings:

1 pint jelly tablet (greengage or lemon)	1 Swiss roll (filled with greengage or raspberry jam)
½ pint water or fruit syrup	¼ pint evaporated milk

To decorate:

few rings canned pineapple	few glacé cherries angelica

1 Dissolve the jelly in ½ pint boiling water or fruit syrup.
2 Put a good half of this on one side to add to evaporated milk.
3 Using a round cake tin, 6 × 3 inches, set a thin layer of remaining jelly on the bottom.
4 When set, arrange the well-drained halved rings of pineapple and glacé cherries and leaves of angelica on the set jelly and add a little more liquid jelly, set this.
5 Cut the Swiss roll in slices about ¾-inch thick.
6 Brush with the cold jelly and press round sides of the cake tin.
7 Allow these to set.
8 Whisk up the evaporated milk until stiff, pour in the remaining jelly and whisk again making a mousse-like texture.
9 Pour the mousse into the middle of the lined cake tin and leave to set for 2–3 hours.
10 To turn out, dip bottom of tin in hot water to loosen jelly and turn out on to a plate.

Caramel meat loaf

cooking time: 1 hour

you will need for 8 servings:

1½ lb. minced beef	2 eggs
12 oz. minced ham, or boiled bacon	½ teaspoon dry mustard
4 oz. stale bread	1–2 oz. brown sugar
½ pint milk	3–4 cloves

1 Mince beef and ham together with fine cutter, after they have been minced separately.
2 Break up the bread and soak in the milk for a few minutes.
3 Beat the eggs with the mustard and add to bread and milk.
4 Add this mixture to the meat, mixing well.
5 Spread brown sugar in the bottom of a mould, sprinkle in the whole cloves, then pack in the meat mixture firmly.
6 Bake in a moderately hot oven (400°F.–Gas Mark 5) for 1 hour. Serve hot or cold.

Variation

Piquant meat loaf – grease the tin well, and coat with soft breadcrumbs, omit the sugar. Add a finely grated onion, a little chopped parsley, and a good pinch of mixed herbs to the beef.

Raspberry melon delight

cooking time: few minutes

you will need for 8 servings:

1 honeydew melon	2 oz. sugar
1 lb. raspberries OR	¼ oz. cornflour
2 packets frozen	little castor sugar
raspberries	

1 Cut the melon lengthwise and remove the seeds.
2 If liked, the melon can be cut into a vandyke shape.
3 Make a sauce by simmering 4 oz. of the raspberries with little water and sugar until tender.
4 Rub through a sieve and make the purée up to ½ pint with water, if necessary.
5 Mix the cornflour smoothly with a little of the purée and put the rest on to heat.
6 Add the mixed cornflour and cook for 3 minutes, stirring constantly.
7 Leave to get quite cold.
8 Pile the remaining raspberries into the melon shell, putting a few round the base for decoration.
9 Pour the cold sauce over and sprinkle with castor sugar, chill well before serving.

After Theatre Supper Parties

It is often easier to have a meal after going to the theatre or cinema, which means it must be left cooking, ready to eat some time later.

The simple menus in this chapter are very interesting, will not be spoiled by people arriving a little later than envisaged, and yet have an air of luxury and party atmosphere.

They are reasonably easy to digest, which is important for a meal served very late at night. Notes have been given in menus as to how dishes may be prepared earlier and kept ready for a late supper.

Have the table set for arrival and the coffee tray laid, so only the last minute finishing touches remain before the meal is ready.

Ham and grapefruit special

no cooking

you will need for 6 servings:

6 prunes	1–1¼ lb. cooked bacon
3 grapefruit	or ham

For dressing:

4 dessertspoons grapefruit juice	freshly ground black pepper
about ½ teaspoon continental mustard	4 dessertspoons corn or olive oil
about ½ teaspoon salt	1–2 dessertspoons lemon juice

To garnish:

1 bunch watercress	few walnuts

1 Steam or cook prunes, until just plump, in a little water, then strain and remove stones.
2 Divide two of the grapefruit, cutting the skin in zigzag (vandyke) fashion.
3 Remove flesh from halves and blend with some juice of the third grapefruit.
4 To make the dressing, mix four dessertspoons of the grapefruit juice with the mustard, salt and freshly ground black pepper, beat in the corn or olive oil and sharpen well with lemon juice.
5 Toss the grapefruit sections and prunes in the dressing, mix with ham, pile into grapefruit cups and garnish with fresh watercress and walnuts. Cover with foil for a late supper to prevent drying.

Rich trifle

no cooking

you will need for 6 servings:

4 individual sponge cakes	1 oz. blanched and shredded almonds
raspberry or strawberry jam	½ pint custard, see page 29
6 macaroons	¼ pint thick cream
12 ratafia biscuits	1 egg white
¼ pint sherry	1–2 oz. castor sugar
grated rind ½ lemon	

To decorate:

glacé cherries	angelica

1 Split the sponge cakes in two and spread lower halves with jam, replace tops.
2 Arrange in a glass dish and cover with macaroons and ratafias.
3 Soak with sherry and sprinkle with lemon rind and almonds.

4 Cover with the custard and leave to cool.
5 Whisk the cream, egg-white and sugar together until stiff and pile on top of the trifle.
6 Decorate with glacé cherries and angelica.

Variation
Banana rum trifle – heat 2 oz. sugar and 2 tablespoons rum, until a golden brown syrup. Add 3–4 sliced bananas and cook until the bananas absorb the syrup. Split the sponge cakes as in the recipe above and sandwich with this rich mixture instead of jam. Add the macaroons, ratafias and 2 tablespoons rum blended with 2 tablespoons sweetened lemon juice. Continue as the rich trifle recipe.

Burgundy beef in red wine

cooking time: 2¼ hours

you will need for 4 servings:

1½ lb. stewing beef, cut into cubes	2 oz. mushrooms, peeled and sliced
½ oz. seasoned flour	pinch sugar
1 oz. dripping or fat	¼ pint red wine, scant measure
2 rashers streaky bacon, cut into pieces	½ pint stock
	seasoning
12 small onions	*bouquet garni*

To serve:
parsley   creamed potatoes

1 Roll cubes of beef in seasoned flour, brown well on all sides in melted dripping, remove from pan.
2 Add bacon, onions, mushrooms and sugar and brown gently again.
3 Remove mushrooms and onions, return the meat.
4 Heat the wine, add to meat, add stock to cover.
5 Add seasoning and *bouquet garni*, cover and cook slowly for 1 hour.
6 Add onions and mushrooms and continue cooking for another hour.
7 Serve with chopped parsley and creamed potatoes, see page 48.

Variations
With peppers – for a more colourful casserole add pieces of red and green pepper with the onions.

With potatoes and peas – for a complete casserole meal, use a little extra stock, add tiny potatoes and green peas for the last 30 minutes of the cooking time, adding extra seasoning.

Wine casserole of chicken – use a jointed chicken instead of beef, use red or white wine. If using boiling fowl follow cooking time as beef; if using young chicken, cook for 1¼–1½ hours only, use slightly less stock. For late supper use lower heat and cook for longer period.

Strawberry flan

cooking time: 30 minutes

you will need for 4–6 servings:
6 oz. flan pastry, see page 22.

For filling:
12 oz. strawberries

For glaze:

2 level teaspoons arrowroot	2 oz. castor sugar
½ pint water – flavoured with strawberries	few drops cochineal

To decorate:
¼ pint thick cream

1 Make the pastry and bake 'blind', see page 50, in a deep 8-inch fluted flan ring just above the centre of a moderately hot oven (375°F.–Gas Mark 5) for 15 minutes.
2 Remove the flan from the tin and return to the oven for a further 10–15 minutes. Cool.
3 The strawberries can be put straight into the flan case, or there is more flavour if a syrup is made by boiling the sugar and water, remove from the heat, put in the strawberries, allow to cool, then drain.
4 Make sure the strawberries are quite cold, in this case, before they go into the pastry.
5 Blend the arrowroot with the water and sugar, (or syrup if made beforehand as suggested above).
6 Add 2 or 3 drops cochineal to give a pleasant pink colour, boil until thick and clear, stirring all the time.
7 Allow this glaze to cool, then spread with a palette knife or brush over the strawberries.
8 Decorate with whipped cream.

Variation
Mixed fruit flan – use canned fruit, drain well, and use ¼ pint syrup from can.

Cheese and ham loaf

cooking time: 10 minutes

you will need for 4 servings:

1 lb. tomatoes
1 tablespoon chopped chives
1 pint chicken stock
½ oz. powdered gelatine
2 tablespoons water
1 tablespoon salad cream or mayonnaise
2 tablespoons cream
4 oz. cream cheese
8 oz. chopped cooked ham
1 teaspoon chopped parsley
seasoning

1 Chop the tomatoes. Add chives.
2 Cook in the stock until pulpy. Rub through a sieve.
3 Dissolve the gelatine in the water and stir into the tomato juice.
4 Pour into a ring mould to set.
5 Mix together the salad cream and cream and stir in the cheese, ham, parsley and seasoning.
6 Turn out the mould and fill the centre with the cheese mixture.

To prevent drying for a late supper party, either turn out at the last minute or have ready turned out and cover completely with foil.

Mallow prune tarts

cooking time: 30 minutes

you will need for 12 tarts:
8 oz. short crust pastry, see page 72

For filling:

8 oz. prunes
½ pint boiling water
grated rind ½ orange
1½ oz. castor sugar
1 level tablespoon arrowroot
juice ½ orange
juice 1 lemon

To decorate:
12 dessert marshmallows

1 Make the pastry and line twelve bun tins with 3-inch rounds of pastry.
2 Prick well and bake in a hot oven (425–450°F. –Gas Mark 6–7) for 10–12 minutes until crisp and golden.
3 Soak the prunes in boiling water for 1 hour. Drain, but reserve liquid.

4 Stone and chop the prunes, then put into a pan with the reserved liquid, orange rind and the sugar.
5 Simmer for 20 minutes.
6 Mix the arrowroot to a smooth paste with the orange and lemon juice, then add to the prune mixture.
7 Cook, stirring until the mixture comes to the boil, and thickens, then simmer for 3 minutes.
8 Remove cool pastry cases from tins and fill with the warm prune mixture.
9 Put a whole marshmallow on the top of each and return to the oven for ½–1 minute, or until the marshmallows brown and melt slightly.

For a late supper party prepare to stage 8, then reheat for about 10 minutes, putting marshmallows on top for the last minute.

Veal paprika or goulash

cooking time: 1½–2 hours

you will need for 4 servings:

8 oz. onions
2 tomatoes
1–1½ lb. stewing veal
1 oz. fat
1 clove garlic, optional
½ oz. paprika pepper
½ oz. flour
½–¾ pint water or stock
1 beef bouillon cube
salt, pepper
¾ pint yoghourt

1 Slice the onions and skin the tomatoes.
2 Cut meat into 1-inch cubes and brown quickly in hot fat.
3 Remove the meat from fat and fry the sliced onions and crushed garlic slightly.
4 Add paprika pepper and flour and stir over a low heat.
5 Pour in the stock and bouillon cube and bring slowly to the boil, stirring.
6 Return the meat to the liquid, add the chopped tomatoes, season, and simmer gently for 1½–2 hours.
7 Just before serving stir in most of the yoghourt.
8 Put into hot dish and top with remaining yoghourt.

When leaving for a late supper, proceed to stage 6, but put into casserole and leave at 285°F. or Gas Mark 1 for about 3–4 hours.

Passion fruit fluff

no cooking

you will need for 4 servings:

¼ pint whipped thick cream or evaporated milk
3 level dessertspoons gelatine
3 tablespoons water
6 passion fruit OR ½ pint canned passion fruit pulp
grated rind and juice 1 lemon
2 oz. sugar
3 eggs

1 Chill the cream or evaporated milk.
2 Soften the gelatine in the cold water and dissolve over boiling water. Cool.
3 Put the passion fruit, lemon juice, sugar and egg yolks into a bowl.
4 Stir over boiling water until the mixture thickens. Cool.
5 Add the gelatine and lemon rind, leave till partly set.
6 Fold in the whipped cream.
7 Beat the egg whites stiffly and stir into the mixture.
8 Put into a mould or glasses to set.

Variation

Raspberry fluff - use about 1 lb. sieved fresh or firm cooked fruit - raspberries are ideal, but strawberries, blackcurrants or gooseberries, can be used.

Kidney, bacon and mushroom pie

cooking time: 55 minutes

you will need for 4 servings:

12 oz. lamb's kidneys
8 oz. bacon
fat for frying
8 oz. mushrooms
1 onion
2 teaspoons flour
¼ pint stock
salt and pepper
6–8 oz. flaky pastry, see page 64
little milk

1 Skin and halve kidneys, cut bacon into strips.
2 Fry in pan, then put layers of bacon, kidneys, and sliced mushrooms into a pie dish.
3 Add sliced onion to the fat in the pan and cook until soft.
4 Stir in flour, cook for 2–3 minutes.
5 Add stock, seasoning, bring to the boil and cook until thickened.
6 Pour into the pie dish, top with pastry and glaze over with milk.

7 Bake in the centre of a very hot oven (450–475°F.–Gas Mark 7–8) for 15–20 minutes, then reduce heat to moderate (375°F.–Gas Mark 4) for the rest of the time.
8 Serve with creamed or Duchesse potatoes, see page 46, baked tomatoes, green vegetables, or salad.
9 This can be served cold with salad.

Variations

With chicken – use the same recipe, adding jointed young frying chicken instead of kidneys – allow little longer cooking time.

With liver – use strips of calves' liver instead of kidneys.

For a late supper, cook earlier and reheat for about 25 minutes in a moderately hot oven (400°F.–Gas Mark 5).

Apricot caramel dream

cooking time: few minutes

you will need for 6–8 servings:

4 oz. granulated or loaf sugar
4 tablespoons water
1 × 16 oz. can apricots
3 level tablespoons cornflour
2 oz. butter
vanilla essence
½ pint thick cream
1 dessertspoon castor sugar
2–3 tablespoons toasted coconut

1 Put sugar and water in a heavy saucepan. Stir until the sugar has dissolved, allow mixture to come to the boil and simmer, until the caramel becomes a rich amber colour.
2 Drain juice from apricots and make up to 1 pint with water.
3 Blend the cornflour with a little of the apricot juice and add the remainder of the juice to the caramel, stirring well over heat until blended.
4 Pour the hot liquid on to the cornflour, stirring all the time. Return to pan and bring to the boil. Cook for 2 minutes until smooth and thickened.
5 Remove from the heat and stir in the butter and a few drops vanilla essence.
6 Pour the caramel into a serving bowl, cool, then arrange the apricot halves on the top.
7 Beat the cream until thick, add the castor sugar.
8 Decorate with cream and coconut.

Avocado with chicken salad

no cooking

you will need for 4 servings:

1 orange	4 tablespoons
12 oz. cooked, diced	mayonnaise
chicken	pinch salt
½ chopped green	2 avocado pears
pepper	1½ tablespoons lemon
1–2 oz. slivered	juice
blanched almonds	

To serve:

mayonnaise   lettuce

1 Cut the orange into sections and mix with the chicken, pepper, almonds, mayonnaise and salt. Chill.
2 Just before serving, cut avocados in half and sprinkle with lemon juice.
3 Fill with the chicken salad, and serve with mayonnaise and lettuce.

For an after theatre supper party, prepare the filling earlier, keep covered with foil and put into avocado halves at last minute.

Cheesecake

cooking time: 50 minutes

you will need for 4 servings:

*short crust pastry,	2 oz. butter or
see page 72, made	margarine
with:	good pinch salt
4 oz. flour	water or egg yolk to
	mix

For filling:

3 oz. butter or	12 oz. cottage or
margarine	cream cheese
2 oz. castor sugar	2 tablespoons thin
2 eggs	cream or top of milk

*Or use biscuit crumbs as recipe, page 34.

1 Line a 7-inch pie plate with wafer-thin pastry or biscuit crumbs.
2 Cream butter and sugar until light and fluffy, gradually beat in the eggs, the cheese and finally the cream.
3 Put into the pastry and set for about 10 minutes in a hot oven (425–450°F.–Gas Mark 6–7), then lower the heat to moderate (325–350°F.–Gas Mark 3) and continue cooking approximately for a further 40 minutes.

Variations

Lemon cheesecake – add the grated rind of 1–2 lemons and 2 tablespoons of lemon juice in place of cream.

Sultana cheesecake – add 1 oz. cornflour at stage 2, after putting in the eggs. Add the cheese, 3 oz. well-plumped sultanas and omit the cream.

Savoury cheesecake – less well known but very delicious is a savoury cheesecake. Omit the sugar, add very tiny pieces of chopped red and green pepper and chopped chives.

Choosing Wines

The most important thing is to choose the wine that you and your guests will enjoy. There is far too much dogma about 'you *must* serve a red wine with certain meat and game', and 'you *must* serve a white wine with fish'. Some people only like a white wine, some people prefer a red. On the whole, though, a lighter wine is ideal to serve with less strong flavoured food, and a red wine complements food that has plenty of taste.

White wine should be served cool. This does not mean it should be iced, because too much flavour is taken from it. You may have a very cool cellar, but if it is kept in a relatively warm place, a short time in a refrigerator will improve it. Red wine should be served at room temperature, and the heavier the red wine, the better it is to leave it standing with the cork withdrawn, so that it has time to become warm and mature in flavour.

Prices of wines

Prices of wines vary enormously. One can buy a favourite wine, such as a Graves or a Chablis, very cheaply, but the really special Graves or Chablis will be considerably more expensive. If you are not very knowledgeable about wines, take time to shop and make a friend of the assistants in the wine stores, who generally are only too happy to give you really good advice.

The aperitif

Before guests sit down to the meal they will probably like an aperitif. They may choose spirits, but most people who enjoy wine with a meal appreciate that this is inclined to spoil their taste later, and will choose therefore a sherry or a vermouth, sweet or dry.

The first course

Often people will prefer to have another sherry or vermouth with their soup; or you may care to open with a white wine. These white wines are ideal to serve at the beginning of a meal, because they help to sharpen the appetite, as they are dry.

Type	Name
Bordeaux	Graves
Burgundy	Pouilly-Fuissé
Burgundy	Meursault
Burgundy	Chablis
Burgundy	Puligny-Montrachet

The above wines are also extremely suitable to serve with veal and many people will enjoy them with chicken. They are ideal to serve with fish, whether as the main or the first course.

The main course

For the main course, if you still wish to serve a white wine, any of the above are a good choice, or try some of the Loire wines or hocks given below.

Type	Name
Loire	Blanc Fumé de Pouilly
Loire	Château du Nozet
Hock	Riesling
Hock	Liebfraumilch
Hock	Oppenheimer
Hock	Niersteiner
Hock	Deinsheimer

A sparkling hock makes a pleasant change. Some of the Australian Riesling type wines are an excellent choice for a white wine.
Or you could choose an Italian Chianti.
If you choose a red wine with your main course, these suit most palates.

Type	Name
Burgundy	Nuits-St. Georges
Burgundy	Beaune
Burgundy	Beaujolais
Burgundy	Volnay
Burgundy	Pommard
Burgundy	Meursault Rouge

A sparkling Burgundy may be liked by some people, but it is very much an acquired taste.

Bordeaux is considered the ideal drink for duck or game. There is a very wide variation in price, the Chateau-bottled being considerably more expensive.

Type	Name
Bordeaux	Medoc
Bordeaux	Pomerol
Bordeaux	St. Emilion
Bordeaux	Margaux

The sweet course

To serve with the sweet course one would choose a sweet white wine.

Type	Name
Bordeaux	Sauternes
	Barsac

Another suggestion would be to serve a vin rosé throughout the meal, or one of the very excellent types of vin rosé listed below.

Name
Graves rosé
Tavel rosé
Mateus rosé

With the fruit and nuts, a port wine; and with coffee one of the many liqueurs such as:– Advocaat, Apricot brandy, Benedictine, Cherry brandy, Crème de Menthe, Kummel and Brandy.

Setting the Table

The look of a table for a dinner or supper party makes a great deal of difference to the meal, for a beautifully laid table immediately looks as though care and thought has been spent.

Flowers

If space permits, have either a low bowl of flowers in the centre of the table, or tiny ones at the corners of a square or rectangular table. Make certain the vase or bowl is heavy so it cannot easily be knocked over, and the flower arrangement sufficiently low so that it does not obstruct people's visibility. Avoid any flowers with a slightly strong or unpleasant smell. Instead of flowers, candles are most effective.

Arranging the cutlery

There are two ways of arranging the cutlery. The first, generally considered the more modern, is to put the knives, forks and spoons in the order in which they will be used. Put the cheese plate in position, to the left of the forks, with napkin, and glass or glasses to the right of the knives.

The other arrangement is to have the dessert spoon and fork over the top of the place setting, the spoon uppermost and pointing towards the forks, and the fork prongs towards the knives. Check to see that the salt, pepper and mustard are filled and the latter freshly made. Even if you are serving wine, have a jug of water, preferably iced, on the sideboard because many people like both wine and water.

Store Cupboard Menus

Very often a busy housewife has little if any warning of entertaining friends to supper or dinner. It probably means she has to make it with those ingredients she had planned for a family meal, plus a few extras in the store cupboard.

The menus in this chapter show how rather ordinary canned or convenience foods, can be utilized to turn the meal into something a little special.

A busy housewife will find menu planning easier if she thinks ahead as much as possible. In order to have food for unexpected guests, try to bake extra meringue shells, a spare pastry flan case. Have available rather interesting canned foods, such as canned cream, chestnut purée, soups like turtle, oxtail and creamed asparagus.

It is often quicker to cook a large piece of meat like gammon, see page 91, the night before you entertain, and just garnish it at the last moment.

Corned beef cutlets

cooking time: 15–20 minutes

you will need for 4 servings:

For sauce:

1 oz. margarine	¼ pint milk or stock
1 oz. flour	
1 packet sage and onion stuffing	salt, pepper
	1 egg
12 oz. corned beef	fat for frying

1 Make the sauce by heating the margarine in the saucepan, stirring in the flour and cooking 2 minutes, then adding the liquid.
2 Bring to the boil and cook until thick.
3 Add half the stuffing, the flaked corned beef, salt and pepper.
4 Form into cutlet shapes, coat with beaten egg and the remainder of the stuffing.
5 Fry in hot fat until crisp and golden brown.

Quick peach dumplings

cooking time: 15–20 minutes

you will need for 4 servings:

4 oz. flour (with plain flour use 1 teaspoon baking powder)
pinch salt
2 oz. finely chopped suet
½ oz. sugar
4 tablespoons milk
1 large can (approximately 1 lb. 13 oz.) peach slices or halves

1 Sift flour and salt into a bowl and add suet and sugar.
2 Mix to a fairly stiff consistency with the milk.
3 With well-floured hands, shape into eight dumplings.
4 Drain fruit, pour syrup into large shallow pan.
5 Bring to boil, then put in the dumplings.
6 Reduce heat, cover pan and poach slowly for 10–15 minutes.
7 Transfer dumplings to a warm serving dish, coat with syrup and decorate with warmed, canned fruit.
8 If you do not wish to open a can of fruit, try poaching the dumplings in a mixture of water and lemon juice sweetened to taste. Dust with sugar before serving.

Asparagus lamb cutlets

cooking time: 55 minutes

you will need for 4 servings:

8 cutlets best end neck lamb
3 oz. butter
2 large onions
1 can asparagus soup
To garnish:
tomatoes
seasoning
little cream or top of milk
1 lb. sliced potatoes

1 Prepare and trim the cutlets.
2 Melt 2 oz. of the butter in a saucepan and cook the sliced onions until golden but not soft, add cutlets and cook for 5 minutes.
3 Place onions and cutlets in a greased casserole.
4 Pour in soup, seasoning lightly, and the cream or top of milk.
5 Top with the thinly sliced, seasoned potatoes and the rest of the butter.
6 Cook for about 50 minutes in the centre of a moderate oven (400°F.–Gas Mark 5).
7 While the casserole is cooking, fry rings of tomatoes and arrange round the edge for garnish.

Orange meringues

cooking time: 3 minutes

you will need for 4 servings:

4 large oranges
block ice cream
2 egg whites
3 oz. sugar

1 Cut a slice from the top of each orange and remove as much of the flesh as possible.
2 Pack back into unbroken orange cases.
3 Top with ice cream.
4 Whisk egg whites until very stiff.
5 Fold in sugar.
6 Pile *over* ice cream – brown for 3 minutes in a very hot oven (475–500°F.–Gas Mark 8–9).

Texas three ring rice

cooking time: 50 minutes

you will need for 4 servings:

2 medium-sized onions
½ green pepper
1 small clove garlic
4 oz. butter or margarine
8 oz. minced beef
1-6 oz. can tomato paste
1 teaspoon salt
½ teaspoon chilli powder
⅛ teaspoon pepper
1 red pepper
8 oz. cooked rice
1 packet frozen peas
1 can tomato soup
2 hardboiled eggs chopped
Parmesan cheese

1 Chop onions and green pepper, mince garlic.
2 Fry in half the butter until tender.
3 Add minced beef and cook until brown.
4 Stir in tomato paste and seasonings.
5 Cut red pepper into strips.
6 Arrange attractively in the bottom of a ring mould.
7 Combine rice and rest of melted butter and spoon into mould.
8 Top with cooked peas, then beef mixture.
9 Press each layer firmly with back of spoon.
10 Set mould in a shallow pan of hot water.
11 Bake in centre of a very moderate oven (350°F. –Gas Mark 3) for 30–40 minutes. Turn out on to a plate.
12 In a small saucepan heat tomato soup. Add hardboiled eggs.
13 Serve over mould and sprinkle with Parmesan cheese.

Mock pumpkin pie

cooking time: approximately 1½ hours

you will need for 6 servings:

8 oz. short crust pastry, see page 72

1½–2 lb. very young parsnips

4 oz. sugar
just under ½ pint milk
1 teaspoon vanilla essence
2 eggs
3 oz. castor sugar

To decorate:
few glacé cherries   blanched almonds

1 Make pastry and line a deep 8–9-inch flan tin.
2 Press pastry firmly into tin and DO NOT prick.
3 Peel and cook sufficient parsnips, without salt, to yield 12 oz.–1 lb. when cooked.
4 Wash or sieve free from lumps and add sugar, milk and vanilla essence.
5 Separate the eggs and beat the yolks into the parsnip mixture.
6 Place in the flan case and bake in a moderately hot oven (400°F.–Gas Mark 5) for approximately 40 minutes.
7 Make meringue, see page 24, with egg whites and castor sugar.
8 Place on top of the pie, swirling into peaks and return to a slow oven (275–300°F.–Gas Mark 1–2) for 15 minutes until tinted golden brown.
9 Decorate with a few glacé cherries and blanched almonds.

Swiss steak special

cooking time: 1¼ hours

you will need for 4 servings:

2 oz. butter
clove garlic, optional
1 packet onion soup mix
1 lb. rump steak, 1-inch thick

little black pepper
3 tablespoons red wine
4 oz. mushrooms

1 Spread 1 oz. of the butter over the centre of a piece of foil 15 × 15 inches double thickness, halve garlic, rub over foil.
2 Sprinkle half the packet of soup, after shaking well, over the butter. Place steak on this.
3 Sprinkle a little black pepper on the steak, then the remainder of the soup mix.
4 Pour the wine over this.
5 Slice mushrooms and arrange round the steak.

6 Fold the foil and make into a parcel to prevent juices running out.
7 Bake for approximately 1¼ hours in centre of a hot oven (450°F.–Gas Mark 7).
8 Serve with boiled rice and a green vegetable.

Baked Alaska

cooking time: 3 minutes

you will need for 4 servings:

large block vanilla ice cream*
little frozen fruit, canned OR fresh fruit

5 egg whites
8 oz. sugar

*This must be rock-hard, so purchase at last minute and store carefully.

1 Put the block of ice cream on to an ovenproof dish.
2 It can be put over a square of sponge cake if wished.
3 Arrange the well-drained fruit round the ice cream.
4 Whip up the egg whites until very stiff.
5 Fold in the sugar.
6 Pile over the ice cream and fruit until completely covered and brown for 3 minutes only in a very hot oven (475–500°F.–Gas Mark 8–9).

Corned beef Scotch eggs

cooking time: 8–10 minutes

you will need for 4–6 servings:

For the sauce:
1 oz. margarine
1 oz. flour

¼ pint milk or stock

12 oz. corned beef
4 oz. breadcrumbs
seasoning
6 hardboiled eggs

1 egg
crisp breadcrumbs
fat for frying

1 To make the sauce heat the margarine in a saucepan, stir in the flour and cook for 2 minutes, then add the liquid.
2 Stir until boiling, cook until thick.
3 Add the breadcrumbs and the flaked corned beef, season well.
4 Press the mixture round the outside of the shelled hardboiled eggs.
5 When you have a neat shape, brush with beaten egg, toss carefully in breadcrumbs, fry until crisp and golden brown in heated fat.

Chocolate orange mousse

no cooking

you will need for 4 servings:
2 oz. chocolate
2 eggs

finely grated rind
1 orange

To decorate:
about 12 orange
  segments

little thick cream

1 Melt chocolate in a basin over hot water.
2 Add the egg yolks and orange rind, and stir into the melted chocolate.
3 Beat the whites until stiff and fold into the mixture.
4 Pour into dishes and decorate with orange segments and rosettes of whipped cream using a No. 6 or 8 star pipe.

Gammon and peaches

cooking time: approximately 3 hours

you will need for 12–15 servings:
5–6 lb. boned gammon
  joint
1 medium-sized can
  sliced peaches
cucumber

1 glass sherry
4 tablespoons peach
  syrup
1 teaspoon arrowroot

To serve:
salad

cucumber

1 Soak the joint overnight.
2 Either cook by simmering, allowing approximately 35–40 minutes per lb. and 35–40 minutes over; or simmer for half the time and bake in a very moderate oven (300–350°F.–Gas Mark 2-3) for the rest.
3 When the gammon is tender, strip off the skin, and when cold arrange peach slices in a daisy pattern on the fat, using cucumber skin for stem and leaves.
4 Put the sherry and peach syrup into a pan and bring to boil.
5 Add blended arrowroot and boil until thick, allow to cool slightly and spoon over the top of the gammon.
6 Serve with salad and cucumber.

Hawaiian rings

no cooking

you will need for 4 servings:
4 rings canned
  pineapple
4 portions coffee ice
  cream

small can raspberries
small can mandarin
  orange slices

1 Set the pineapple rings on four flat plates.
2 Put a spoonful of coffee ice cream in the centre covering the hole.
3 Alternate round the edge with raspberries and mandarin oranges to form a flower.

Curried beef

cooking time: 30–35 minutes

you will need for 4–6 servings:
1 onion, finely
  chopped
2 tablespoons oil
1 lb. raw minced beef
1 level dessertspoon
  mixed herbs
1 egg
1 oz. cornflour

1 packet soup, curry
  flavoured*
1¼ pints water
2 tablespoons sherry
12 oz. cooked mashed
  potatoes†
1 lb. peas

*Other soups can be used, so changing the title of the dish – i.e. tomato, mushroom, etc.
†Or use 6–8 oz. cooked rice, see page 51.

1 Fry the onion in the heated oil.
2 Remove from the pan and mix with the beef, herbs and egg.
3 Form the mixture into balls and coat lightly with the cornflour.
4 Return the meat balls to the pan and brown in the remaining oil. Remove from pan.
5 Add soup, water and wine. Bring to the boil. Stir well.
6 Replace meat balls, cover and simmer gently for 20–25 minutes.
7 Line a large ovenproof dish with the mashed potato and pipe a decorative edge.
8 Brush potato with a little milk and brown under the grill. Heat the peas.
9 Pile the meat balls in the centre of the potato with a little of the sauce. Surround with peas. Serve the remaining sauce separately.

Coffee cream mousse

cooking time: few minutes

you will need for 4–6 servings:

1 oz. cornflour	¾ pint milk
1 level tablespoon cocoa	2 eggs
2½ level dessertspoons instant coffee	½ oz. gelatine
3 tablespoons hot water	
3 oz. castor sugar	¼ pint thick cream

To decorate:
thick cream

1 Mix the cornflour, cocoa, coffee and 1 oz. sugar with a little of the cold milk.
2 Put the rest on to heat.
3 Pour on to the mixed cornflour, return to the saucepan, bring to the boil and cook for 3 minutes, stirring constantly.
4 Add beaten egg yolks and cook for several minutes without boiling.
5 Remove from the heat and add the gelatine dissolved in the hot water and allow to cool.
6 Beat the egg whites stiffly, then beat in the remaining 2 oz. sugar.
7 Fold cream into the cooked mixture together with egg whites and pour into a wetted 1¾–2 pint mould.
8 When set decorate with more cream.

Rice chowder

cooking time: 40 minutes

you will need for 4 servings:

2 oz. rice	2 bay leaves
1¾ pints water	4 oz. diced potatoes
salt, pepper	2 oz. diced bacon

1 Put the rice into the seasoned water.
2 Bring to the boil and cook for 10 minutes.
3 Add the bay leaves, potatoes and bacon.
4 Cook for a further 30 minutes, remove bay leaves and serve.

Savoury omelettes

cooking time: about 10 minutes

you will need for 4 servings:

4 oz. cooked ham or pork or chicken	2 oz. bean sprouts, chopped
1 tiny onion	¼ teaspoon salt
2 oz. chestnuts,* chopped	5 eggs, well beaten
	fat or oil for frying

*Or canned water chestnuts or green beans.

1 Mince or chop all the ingredients together except the salt and eggs, fat or oil.
2 Add salt and eggs, beating until thick.
3 Drop spoonfuls into hot fat and fry for approximately 10 minutes, turning to brown on either side.

Marron glacé torte

cooking time: 2 hours

you will need for 4 servings:
meringue made with 1 egg white, see page 24

To decorate:

4–5 level tablespoons chestnut purée	1 large block strawberry and vanilla ice cream
a few almonds, blanched and halved	

1 Make the meringue.
2 Place in a piping bag or syringe with a plain ½-inch meringue pipe, and on a sheet of oiled greaseproof paper placed on a baking sheet, pipe a 'catherine wheel' about 8 inches in diameter.
3 Set in a cool oven (225–250°F.–Gas Mark 0–½) for approximately 2 hours until dry.
4 Place the meringue base on a serving dish and with a piping bag or syringe and a ½-inch star meringue pipe, make rosettes of chestnut purée round the edge of the meringue base.
5 Decorate with the almonds and spoon the ice cream into the centre.

Tomato Swiss steak

cooking time: 2 hours

you will need:

1¼–1½ lb. stewing steak	1 pint tomato soup or tomato sauce, see page 75
2 tablespoons oil	olives
2 sliced onions	

1 Trim the meat and cut in four portions.
2 Brown well on both sides in oil.
3 Remove the meat to a casserole.
4 Brown the onions in the oil.
5 Place these on top of the meat.
6 Cover meat with soup or sauce.
7 Cook in a moderate oven (375°F.–Gas Mark 4) for about 1¼–2 hours or until meat is tender.
8 Garnish with sliced olives.

Apple dowdy

cooking time: 1 hour

you will need for 4 servings:

1lb. apples	3 cloves
3 oz. sugar	water

Scone dough:

6 oz. flour	½ teaspoon salt
1 level teaspoon cream of tartar	1 dessertspoon sugar milk to mix
½ teaspoon bicarbonate of soda	

1 Pare, core and slice the apples and place in a saucepan.
2 Sprinkle with sugar and cloves, and add water to barely cover.
3 Make scone dough – sieve dry ingredients, blend with milk, form into a round the size of the saucepan.
4 Cover apples with scone dough and cook slowly for 1 hour.
5 Turn out on to a dish, cutting the scone into four pieces and placing them on top of the apples.
6 Serve with cream or delicious creamy lemon sauce, see below.

Creamy lemon sauce

no cooking time

you will need:

1 small tin condensed milk	grated rind and juice 1 lemon

1 Add to the milk the grated rind and lemon juice.
2 Stir well.
3 Serve with Apple dowdy, above, or with steamed sponges.

Corned beef hash

cooking time: 10 minutes

you will need for 4 servings:

12 oz. can corned beef approximately 8 oz. mashed potatoes	1 egg seasoning 1 oz. fat for frying

To garnish and serve:

parsley	cooked beetroot

1 Flake the corned beef and mix with the potatoes and beaten egg.
2 Season well.
3 Heat the fat in a pan and put in the mixture.
4 Spread this evenly and allow to cook slowly until the underside is golden-brown and the mixture really hot.
5 Fold like an omelette and turn on to a hot dish.
6 Garnish with parsley and serve with sliced beetroot.
7 Serve with orange and onion salad below, which gives a pleasant 'bite' to the dish.

Orange and onion salad

no cooking

you will need for 4 servings:

3 oranges	4 oz. black olives
2 medium-sized Spanish onions	2 tablespoons olive oil salt and pepper

1 Peel and slice the oranges very thinly.
2 Slice onions thinly and separate into rings.
3 Stone and chop olives.
4 Mix all ingredients thoroughly together, with the olive oil, and season with salt and pepper.

Fruit cream foule

no cooking

you will need for 4 servings:

¾ pint thick sweetened fruit purée	½ pint thick cream

1 Beat purée until very smooth, or sieve to remove pips and skin.
2 Beat cream until thick.
3 Fold in most of cream, put into glasses.
4 Decorate with cream.
5 Serve as cold as possible.

Index

Alabama sauce with prawns, 31
Alaska, baked, 90
Ale, mulled, 64
Almond horseshoes, 59
Anchovy eggs, 56
Anchovy fingers, 10
Angels on horseback, 16
Apple:
  Apple and blackberry roly poly, 42
  Apple and orange jelly rings, 35
  Apple and prune stuffing, 29
  Apple and raisin stuffing, 17
  Apple cake, 62
  Apple charlotte pie, 15
  Apple dowdy, 93
  Apple gingerbread surprise, 68
  Apple meringue slices, 66
  Apple snowballs, 26
  Apricot glazed apple flan, 12
  Casserole of liver and apples, 49
  French apple flan with redcurrant glaze, 12
  Golden apple pie, 39
  Golden mallow apple pie, 40
  Ham, apple and blue cheese salad, 11
  Love apple pie, 48
  Potato and apple salad, 56
  Stuffed apples, 74
Apricot:
  Apricot and lemon meringue pie, 51
  Apricot and vanilla bavarois, 17
  Apricot caramel dream, 85
  Apricot glazed apple flan, 12
  Apricot meringue pie, 51
  Jellied apricot snow, 27
Artichokes:
  Cold artichokes with vinaigrette dressing, 26
  Globe artichokes, 26
Asparagus:
  To prepare, 27
  Asparagus eggs, 21
  Asparagus lamb cutlets, 89
  Asparagus rolls and ham, 56
Aubergines:
  Scampi Egyptienne, 25
Australian kebabs, 73
Austrian cheese cakes, 48
Avocado pears:
  To prepare, 13
  Avocado and cheese salad, 30
  Avocado and grapefruit salad, 45
  Avocado and shellfish salad, 30
  Avocado with chicken salad, 86

Bacon:
  Bacon and mushroom shells, 79
  Bacon crumb pie, 47
  Bacon salad, 61
  Baked Hawaiian gammon, 79
  Devils on horseback, 16
  Festive bacon, 31
  Gammon and peaches, 91
  Honey peach gammon, 79
  Kidney, bacon and mushroom pie, 85
  Sausage and bacon surprise, 41
Baked Alaska, 90
Baked Hawaiian gammon, 79
Baked mushrooms, 47
Baked stuffed tomatoes, 76
Bakewell tart, 72
Balmoral tartlets, 58
Bamboo shoots with fish and mushrooms, 46
Banana and orange jelly ring, 36
Banana crispies, 78
Banana dessert cake, 67
Banana rum trifle, 83
Barbecue chicken, 71
Barbecued potatoes, 71
Barbecue sauce, 73
Beef:
  Beef darioles, 58
  Burgundy beef in red wine, 83
  Cheese-topped steaks, 15
  Crusted savoury steaks, 13
  Curried beef, 91
  Pieburger, 70
  Saturday cheeseburgers, 68
  Steak with pineapple and cherries, 12
  Swiss steak special, 90
  Tomato Swiss steak, 92
Berry fruit meringue pie, 51

Biscuits:
  Biscuit crumbs crust, 52
  Brandy snaps, 69
  Cheese biscuit pastry, 10
  Pepperpot nut sticks, 68
Blackberry roly poly, 42
Blackberry and apple roly poly 42
Blancmange:
  Coffee macaroon blancmange with chocolate sauce, 80
  Boiled rice, 51
Boned stuffed shoulder of lamb, 16
Braised duck and cherries, 32
Brandy snaps, 69
Bread:
  To prepare, 54
  Bread sauce, 37
  Crusty French wedges, 65
Brown French onion soup, 39
Burgundy beef in red wine, 83
Butter cream, 7

Cabbage:
  Cole slaw, 61
Cacciatore, chicken, 28
Cakes:
  Almond horseshoes, 59
  Apple cake, 62
  Apple gingerbread surprise, 68
  Austrian cheese cakes, 48
  Banana dessert cake, 67
  Cheesecake, 86
  Chocolate pear suprême, 76
  Eccles cakes, 69
  Gâteau suprême, 60
  Grape gâteau, 24
  Pavlova cake, 52
  Sponge, 60
  Uncooked cheesecake, 34
Casseroles and Stews:
  Burgundy beef in red wine, 83
  Casserole of duck, 39
  Casserole of guinea fowl and prunes, 39
  Casserole of liver and apples, 49
  Chinese lamb stew, 18
  Haddock casserole, 48
  Paprika pork casserole, 21
  Wine casserole of chicken, 83
Celeriac and tomato prelude, 20
Celery and crab canapés, 18
Celery bread, 74
Celery, stuffed, 10
Celery stuffing, 17
Cheese:
  To serve, 9
  Anchovy fingers with cheese, 10
  Austrian cheese cakes, 48
  Cheese and avocado salad, 30
  Cheese and ham loaf, 84
  Cheese and Marmite whirls, 10
  Cheese and tomato slices on toast, 77
  Cheese biscuit pastry, 10
  Cheesecake, 86
  Cheese canapés, 10
  Cheese croûtons, 36
  Cheese darioles, 58
  Cheese dip, 71
  Cheese quoits, 67
  Cheese straws, 10
  Cheese-topped steaks, 15
  Corn rarebit, 78
  Ham and cheese on toast, 77
  Kipper cheese spread, 77
  Lemon cheesecake, 86
  Saturday cheeseburgers, 68
  Sultana cheesecake, 86
  Tomato and Parmesan anchovy fingers, 11
  Uncooked cheesecake, 34
  Walnut cheese balls, 66
  Welsh rarebit, 78
  York rarebit, 78
Chef's salad, 61
Cherries:
  Braised duck and cherries, 32
  Fresh cherry vacherin, 47
  Steak with pineapple and cherries, 12
Chestnut stuffing, 37
Chicken:
  Barbecue chicken, 71
  Chicken and mushrooms, 34
  Chicken and rice pompoms, 66
  Chicken blanquette, 27
  Chicken cacciatore with rice, 28
  Chicken liver en surprise, 11

Chicken pâté, 16
Chicken risotto, 53
Chicken vol-au-vent, 35
Chicken with sweet-sour sauce, 42
Chicken with walnuts, 51
Devilled grilled chicken, 50
Grilled chicken, 50
Lemon grilled chicken, 50
Mushroom stuffed chicken legs, 22
Rice with chicken livers, 53
Stuffed chicken legs, 22
Wine casserole of chicken, 83
Chiffon surprise, deloraine, 20
Chinese lamb stew, 18
Chocolate:
  Chocolate and vanilla bavarois, 18
  Chocolate mallow, 70
  Chocolate meringue, 66
  Chocolate orange mousse, 91
  Chocolate pear cream tart, 76
  Chocolate pear suprême, 76
  Chocolate rum mousse, 24
  Chocolate sauce, 80
Chowder, rice, 92
Christmas pudding, 38
Cider cup, 63
Cider cup, sleigh ride, 63
Cling peach pie, 20
Coconut stuffed fruit, 58
Cod's roe pâté, 23
Coffee:
  To serve, 9
  Coffee cornflake flan, 49
  Coffee cream mousse, 92
  Coffee honeycomb mould, 57
  Coffee macaroon blancmange with chocolate sauce, 80
Cole slaw, 61
Cordon Bleu veal, 25
Corned beef and chutney on toast, 77
Corned beef cutlets, 88
Corned beef hash, 93
Corned beef Scotch eggs, 90
Corn rarebit, 78
Cornflake flan, coffee, 49
Crab and avocado salad, 30
Crab and celery canapés, 19
Crab and pineapple cocktails, 18
Cranberry sauce, 37
Cream:
  Cream dressing, 19
  Cream mincemeat tarts, 57
  Cream of asparagus soup, 29
  Cream of mushroom soup, 29
  Cream of tomato soup, 36
  Creamed fish flan, 46
  Creamed meat spread on toast, 27
  Creamed pâté, 16
  Creamed potato croquettes, 26
  Creamed potatoes, 48
  Creamy fish scallops, 49
  Creamy French onion soup, 39
  Creamy lemon sauce, 93
  Creamy pumpkin pie, 38
  Butter cream, 7
  Eastern cream, 44
  Evaporated milk cream, 7
  Fruit cream foule, 93
  Lightened cream, 7
  Mock cream, 7
Creole, double decker, 74
Crispy fried noodles, 51
Crispy herring roes on toast, 77
Crispy Russian salad, 62
Croquettes, potatoes, 26
Croûtons, 36
Croûtons, cheese, 36
Crusted savoury steaks, 13
Crusty French wedges, 65
Cucumber sauce, 14
Curried beef, 91
Curried eggs, 21
Curried egg cobbler, 59
Curried egg pie, 58
Custard:
  Egg custard, 12
  Hot custard sauce, 29
  Lemon custard, 19
Date tartlets, 76
Deloraine chiffon surprise, 20
Desserts: see also
  Flans, fruit, jellies, meringues, mousse, pies, puddings, tarts and tartlets, trifle

Apricot and vanilla bavarois, 17
Apricot caramel dream, 85
Baked Alaska, 90
Banana rum trifle, 83
Blackcurrant fluff, 85
Chocolate and vanilla bavarois, 18
Chocolate mallow, 70
Chocolate pear suprême, 76
Coffee honeycomb mould, 57
Coffee macaroon blancmange with chocolate sauce, 80
Deloraine chiffon surprise, 20
Eastern cream, 44
Fresh cherry vacherin, 47
Fruit cream foule, 93
Gooseberry fluff, 85
Harlequin marshmallow pie, 73
Hawaiian rings, 91
Marron glacé torte, 92
Melon with ginger, 32
Passion fruit fluff, 85
Peach and strawberry delight, 62
Pear and grape salad, 80
Raspberry fluff, 85
Raspberry melon delight, 82
Strawberry fluff, 85
Swiss russe, 81
Devilled almonds, 9
Devilled pork spareribs, 20
Devilled sardines, 77
Double decker creole, 74
Dough for scones, 60, 93
Dressings:
  Cream, 19
  Vinaigrette (French), 28
Drinks:
  Cider cup, 63
  Claret cup, 63
  Cold Hallowe'en punch, 63
  Mulled ale, 64
  Sleigh ride cider cup, 63
  Sleigh ride white wine cup, 63
  White wine, 63
  White wine cup, 63
  Vin rosé cup, 63
Duchesse potatoes, 46
Duck:
  Braised duck and cherries, 32
  Casserole of duck, 39
  Duck pâté, 16
Dundee orange tart, 67
Dumplings:
  Peach dumplings and lemon almond sauce, 15
  Quick peach dumplings, 89

Eastern cream, 44
Eccles cakes, 69
Economy soufflé, 35
Eggs:
  Anchovy eggs, 56
  Asparagus eggs, 21
  Corned beef Scotch eggs, 90
  Curried egg cobbler, 59
  Curried egg pie, 58
  Curried eggs, 21
  Egg boats, 67
  Eggs Florentine, 43
  Ham stuffed eggs, 68
  Sardine eggs, 21
  Savoury omlettes, 92
  Stuffed egg salad, 21
Escallop brochettes, 77
Escalopes of veal, 26
Evaporated milk cream, 7

Festive bacon, 31
Figs:
  Parma ham and fresh figs, 24
Fillets of veal milannaise, 24
Fish: see also
  Haddock, sole, etc.
  Cod's roe pâté, 23
  Creamed fish flan, 46
  Creamy fish scallops, 49
  Fish and mushrooms with bamboo shoots, 46
  Fish cream, 55
  Fish dishes on toast, 77
  Fish mayonnaise, 44
  Fish mornay, 45
  Fish mornay flan, 46
  Fish mousse, 61
  Fish scallops, 49
  Fish scallops au gratin, 49
  Fish scallops mornay, 49
  Fish soufflé, 34

Fish with sweet-sour sauce, 42
Mixed fish cocktails, 18
Piquant fish cream, 56
Piquant fish scallops, 49
Shellfish scallops, 49
Flans:
Apricots glazed apple flan, 12
Coffee cornflake flan, 49
Creamed fish flan, 46
Fish mornay flan, 46
French apple flan with redcurrant
glaze, 12
Fresh fruit sponge flan, 33
Mixed fruit flan, 83
Pineapple whip flan, 43
Sponge flan, 33
Strawberry flan, 83
Summer sponge flan, 33
Flaky pastry, 64
Flan pastry, 22
Fleur pastry, 22
Foamy sauce, 23
Forcemeat stuffing, 37
French bread wedges, 65
French onion soup, brown, 39
French onion soup, creamy, 39
Fried crispy noodles, 51
Fried prawns, 42
Fried rice, 51
Fried salmon, 14
Fried scampi, 25
Fruit:
Baked Alaska, 90
Berry fruit meringue pie, 51
Coconut stuffed fruit, 58
Fresh fruit salad, 71
Fruit cream foule, 93
Fruit pies and tarts, 45
Fruit sponge flan, 33
Fruit tarts, 45
Marzipan stuffed fruit, 58
Mixed fruit flan, 83
Passion fruit fluff, 85

Game, roast, 41
Gammon, see also Bacon
Gammon and peaches, 91
Honey peach gammon, 71
Gâteau suprême, 60
Gingerbread:
Apple gingerbread surprise, 68
Ginger orange pudding, 13
Globe artichokes, 86
Golden apple pie, 39
Golden mallow apple pie, 40
Golden rice salad, 61
Goose:
Pâté de foie gras, 16
Gooseberry charlotte pie, 14
Gooseberry meringue pie, 50
Goulash, 84
Grapes:
Grape and pear salad, 80
Grape gâteau, 25
Grapes in summer sponge flan, 33
Grapefruit:
Avocado and grapefruit salad, 45
Grapefruit and shrimp
cocktail, 79
Grapefruit cocktail, 75
Hot grapefruit, 47
Prawn and grapefruit slices, 77
Gravy, 16
Green salad, 52
Greek lemon soup, 22
Grilled chicken, 50
Grilled salmon, 14
Guinea fowl and prune casserole, 39

Haddock:
Haddock casserole, 48
Kedgeree, 54
Parmesan haddock soufflé, 35
Hallowe'en punch, cold, 63
Ham:
Cheese and ham loaf, 84
Ham and asparagus rolls, 56
Ham and cheese on toast, 77
Ham and grapefruit special, 82
Ham, apple and blue cheese
salad, 10
Ham egg boats, 67
Ham en croûte, 13
Ham stuffed eggs, 68
Melon and ham salad, 10
Parma ham and fresh figs, 24
Parma ham and melon, 33
Parma ham and pears, 24

Harlequin cheese dip, 72
Harlequin marshmallow pie, 73
Harlequin rice, 50
Harlequin rice with veal, 23
Hawaiian gammon, 79
Hawaiian rings, 91
Herrings:
Herring roes on toast, 77
Kipper cheese spread, 77
Kipper pâté, 23
Hollandaise sauce, 28
Honeycomb mould, coffee, 57
Honey nut pie, 22
Honey peach pie, 21
Hors-d'oeuvre:
Anchovy eggs, 56
Asparagus, 27
Avocado and grapefruit salad, 45
Avocado pears, 13
Celeriac and tomato prelude, 20
Chicken pâté, 16
Cod's roe pâté, 23
Crab and celery canapés, 19
Creamed pâté, 16
Duck pâté, 16
Fish cream, 55
Fried scampi, 25
Globe artichokes, 26
Grapefruit cocktail, 75
Grapefruit and shrimp cocktail,
79
Hot grapefruit, 47
Liver pâté, 16
Melon with ginger, 32
Mixed fish cocktail, 17
Orange tomato cocktail, 34
Pâté de fois gras, 16
Piquant flavoured pâté, 16
Prawns with Alabama sauce, 31
Prawns with cream cheese
dressing, 31
Prawns with tomato flavoured
mayonnaise, 31
Scampi Egyptienne, 25
Scampi Indienne, 25
Scampi meunière, 25
Scampi Provençale, 25
Hot grapefruit, 47

Ice cream:
Baked Alaska, 90
Fresh cherry vacherin, 47
Hawaiian rings, 91
Marron glacé torte, 92
Italian meringue, 66

Jellies:
Banana and orange jelly ring, 36
Jellied apricot snow, 27
Jelly delight, 79
Jellied greengage snow, 29
Jellied rhubarb snow, 27
Orange and apple jelly ring, 35
Pear jelly ring, 36

Kebabs, 73
Kedgeree, 54
Kidney, bacon and mushroom pie,
85
Kipper cheese spread, 77
Kipper pâté, 23
Kromeskies, pork and bacon, 56

Lamb:
Asparagus lamb cutlets, 89
Boned stuffed shoulder, 16
Chinese lamb stew, 18
Roast lamb, 14
Savoury chops, 80
Lemon:
Creamy lemon sauce, 93
Greek lemon soup, 22
Lemon and strawberry cream
tarts, 76
Lemon cheesecake, 86
Lemon custard, 19
Lightened cream, 7
Lingalonga peach pie, 53
Liver and apple casserole, 49
Liver pâté, 16
Lobster:
To prepare, 41
Lobster Americaine, 41
Lobster and avocado salad, 30
Lobster au gratin, 41
Lobster mornay, 41
Lobster with sweet-sour sauce, 42
Love apple pie, 48

Macaroni:
Fillets of veal milannaise, 24
Mandarin trifle, 30
Marron glacé torte, 92
Madeira sauce, 40
Marsala sauce, 23
Marshmallow:
Chocolate mallow, 70
Golden mallow apple pie, 40
Mallow prune tarts, 84
Marshmallow fingers, 78
Marshmallow plum pie, 73
Marzipan, 58
Marzipan stuffed fruits, 58
Mayonnaise, 44
Mayonnaise, tomato flavoured,
with prawns, 31
Meat: see also Beef, lamb, pork,
veal
Caramel meat loaf, 81
Meat dishes on toast, 77
Meat kebabs, 73
Melon:
Melon and ham salad, 10
Melon and Parma ham, 33
Melon and pork platter, 80
Melon raspberry delight, 82
Melon with ginger, 32
Meringues:
To prepare, 24
Apple meringue slices, 66
Apricot and lemon meringue pie, 51
Apricot meringue pie, 51
Berry fruit meringue pie, 51
Chocolate meringue, 66
Gooseberry meringue pie, 50
Italian meringue, 66
Meringue pumpkin pie, 37
Orange meringue, 89
Pavlova pyramid, 59
Pineapple meringue pie, 51
Plum meringue pudding, 46
Topping for deloraine chiffon
surprise, 20
Mexicorn tartlets, 70
Mincemeat cream tarts, 56
Mincemeat tart, 45
Mint sauce, 14
Mixed fish cocktails, 18
Mocha mousse, 25
Mock cream, 7
Mock pumpkin pie, 90
Mould, coffee honeycomb, 57
Mousse:
Caramel mousse, 32
Chocolate orange mousse, 91
Chocolate rum mousse, 24
Coffee cream mousse, 92
Mocha mousse, 25
Peach mousse, 13
Pineapple and lemon mousse, 14
Salmon mousse, 60
Mulled ale, 64
Mulled claret, 64
Mushrooms:
Baked mushrooms, 47
Chicken with mushroom, 34
Kidney, bacon and mushroom
pie, 85
Mushroom and bacon shells, 79
Mushroom and fish with bamboo
shoots, 46
Mushroom soufflé, 25
Mushroom soup, 22
Mushroom stuffed chicken or
turkey legs, 22

Noodles, fried crispy, 51
Normandy toasts, 78
Nuts:
Devilled almonds, 9
Salted nuts, 9
Spiced nuts, 9

Omelettes, savoury, 92
Onions:
Brown French onion soup, 39
Creamy French onion soup, 39
Onion and orange salad, 93
Onion sauce, 17
Orange:
Banana and orange jelly ring, 36
Caramel oranges, 55
Chocolate orange mousse, 91
Dundee orange tart, 67
Orange and apple jelly ring, 35
Orange and onion salad, 93
Orange caramel pudding, 23

Orange meringues, 89
Oranges in grapefruit cocktail, 75
Orange tomato cocktail, 34

Paprika pork casserole, 21
Paprika pork chops, 19
Parma ham and fresh figs, 24
Parma ham and melon, 32
Parma ham and pears, 24
Parmesan haddock soufflé, 34
Parsnip: in mock pumpkin pie, 90
Passion fruit fluff, 85
Pastry:
Cheese biscuit pastry, 10
Flaky pastry, 64
Flan or fleur pastry, 22
For almond horseshoes, 59
For gooseberry charlotte pie, 14
Puff pastry, 70
Rough puff pastry, 65
Rich short crust pastry, 72
Short crust pastry, 72
Sweet short crust pastry, 72
Pâtés:
Chicken pâté, 16
Cod's roe pâté, 23
Creamed pâté, 16
Duck pâté, 16
Fish cream pâté, 55
Kipper pâté, 23
Liver pâté, 16
Pâté de fois gras, 16
Pâté with veal, 26
Piquant flavoured pâté, 16
Patties piquant, 72
Pavlova cake, 52
Pavlova pyramid, 59
Peaches:
Gammon and peaches, 91
Lingalonga peach pie, 53
Peach and strawberry delight, 62
Peach dumplings, 15
Peach lemon soufflés, 18
Peach mousse, 13
Peach pie, 20
Quick peach dumplings, 89
Stuffed peaches, 58
Pears:
Chocolate pear suprême, 76
Pear and grape salad, 80
Pear jelly ring, 36
Pear trifle, 30
Stuffed pears, 58
Pepperpot nut sticks, 68
Picburgers with salad, 70
Pies:
Apricot meringue pie, 51
Apricot lemon meringue pie, 51
Bacon crumb pie, 47
Berry fruit meringue pie, 51
Cling peach pie, 20
Creamy pumpkin pie, 38
Curried egg pie, 58
Fruit pies and tarts, 45
Golden apple pie, 39
Golden mallow apple pie, 40
Gooseberry charlotte pie, 14
Gooseberry meringue pie, 50
Kidney, bacon and mushroom
pie, 85
Lingalonga peach pie, 53
Love apple pie, 48
Marshmallow plum pie, 73
Meringue pumpkin pie, 38
Mock pumpkin pie, 90
Pineapple meringue pie, 51
Pizza pie, 54
Plate pie, 45
Pumpkin pie, 38
Walnut pie, 21
Pigeons, stuffed, 40
Pineapple:
Baked Hawaiian gammon, 79
Hawaiian rings, 91
Pineapple and cherries, with
steak, 12
Pineapple and lemon mousse, 14
Pineapple croûtes, 78
Pineapple meringue pie, 51
Pineapple pork loaf, 57
Pineapple sauce, 57
Pineapple whip flan, 43
Piquant meat loaf, 81
Piquant patties, 72
Piquant salad, 62
Pizza pie, 54
Plate pie, 45
Plum marshmallow pie, 73

Index

Plum meringue pudding, 46
Pork:
  Belly of pork with barbecued
    potatoes, 71
  Devilled pork spareribs, 20
  Paprika pork casserole, 20
  Paprika pork chops, 19
  Pineapple pork loaf, 57
  Pork and bacon kromeskies, 56
  Pork and melon platter, 80
  Tipsy pork chops, 19
Potatoes:
  Barbecued potatoes, 71
  Creamed potatoes, 48
  Creamed potato croquettes, 26
  Duchesse potatoes, 46
  Game chips, 41
  Potato and apple salad, 56
  Potatoes boulangère, 81
  Potato cakes, 72
  Potato cheese croquettes, 26
  Potato croquettes, 26
  Potatoes Lyonnaise, 81
  Potato salad, 62
  Savoury potato croquettes, 26
  Scalloped potatoes, 47
Prawns:
  Fried prawns, 42
  Prawn and avocado salad, 30
  Prawn and grapefruit slices, 77
  Prawn cocktail, 18
  Prawn risotto, 52
  Prawns with Alabama sauce, 31
  Prawns with cream cheese
    dressing, 31
  Prawns with tomato flavoured
    mayonnaise, 31
Prunes:
  Casserole of guinea fowl and
    prunes, 39
  Devils on horseback, 16
  Marshmallow prune tarts, 84
  Prune and apple stuffing, 29
  Prune and sausage stuffing, 37
  Prunes in ham and grapefruit
    special, 82
  Veal blanquette with prunes, 26
**Puddings: see also Desserts, flans,
    pies, mousse**
  Apple charlotte pie, 15
  Apple dowdy, 93
  Apple snowballs, 26
  Banana dessert cake, 67
  Blackberry roly poly, 42
  Brandy snaps, 68
  Christmas pudding, 38
  Ginger orange pudding, 13
  Honey nut pie, 22
  Honey peach pie, 21
  Orange caramel pudding, 23
  Plum meringue pudding, 28
  Snowden pudding, 28
  Sugar plum ring, 65
  Queen Mab's pudding, 12
  Viennese pudding, 22
  Puff pastry, 70
  Pumpkin creamy pie, 38
  Pumpkin meringue pie, 38
  Pumpkin pie, 38
  Pumpkin pie, mock, 90
  Punch, cold Hallowe'en 63

Queen Mab's pudding, 12
Quick peach dumplings, 89

Raisin and apple stuffing, 17
Raspberry fluff, 85
Raspberry melon delight, 82
Raspberry trifle, 30
Redcurrant glaze on French apple
  flan, 12
Rice:
  To prepare, 28
  Boiled rice, 51
  Chicken and rice pompoms, 66
  Chicken cacciatore with rice, 28
  Fried rice, 51
  Golden rice salad, 61
  Harlequin rice salad, 61
  Rice chowder, 92
  Rice with chicken livers, 53
  Texas three ring rice, 89
Risotto, 53
Roast game, 41
Roast turkey, 36

Rolls:
  Brown rolls, 55
  Cheese rolls, 55
  Floury topped rolls, 55
  Milk rolls, 55
  Oatmeal topped rolls, 55
  Shiny topped rolls, 55
  Wholemeal rolls, 55
Rough puff pastry, 65
Roly poly, blackberry, 42
Roly poly, blackberry and apple, 42
Royal veal, 25
Rum mousse chocolate, 24
Russian salad, 62

Sage and onion stuffing, 17
Salads:
  Avocado and grapefruit salad, 45
  Avocado with chicken salad, 86
  Cheese and avocado salad, 30
  Chef's salad, 61
  Crispy Russian salad, 62
  Golden rice salad, 61
  Green salad, 52
  Ham, apple and blue cheese
    salad, 10
  Melon and ham salad, 10
  Mixed salad, 52
  Orange and onion salad, 93
  Piquant salad, 62
  Potato and apple salad, 93
  Potato salad, 62
  Russian salad, 62
  Salad egg boats, 67
  Shellfish and avocado salad, 30
  Stuffed egg salad, 21
  Winter salad, 52
Salmon:
  Fried salmon, 14
  Grilled salmon, 14
  Grilled salmon with sauce, 14
  Salmon and fish mould, 44
  Salmon cream, 56
  Salmon mayonnaise, 43
  Salmon mousse, 60
  Salmon steak au gratin, 45
  Salmon steak mornay, 44
  Smoked salmon 12
Salted nuts, 9
Sardines:
  Devilled sardines on toast, 77
  Sardine eggs, 21
Saturday cheeseburgers, 68
Sauces:
  Keeping sauces hot, 5
  Alabama sauce, 31
  Barbecue sauce, 73
  Bread sauce, 37
  Brown sauce, 40
  Chocolate sauce, 80
  Cranberry sauce, 37
  Cream brandy sauce, 38
  Cream sauce, 38
  Creamy lemon sauce, 93
  Cucumber sauce, 14
  Custard sauce, 29
  Foamy sauce, 23
  Hollandaise sauce, 28
  Madeira sauce, 40
  Marsala sauce, 23
  Mint sauce, 14
  Lemon almond sauce, 15
  Onion sauce, 17
  Pineapple sauce, 57
  Sherry sauce, 23
  Sherry cream sauce, 38
  Spanish sauce, 17
  Tangy barbecue sauce, 73
  Tartare sauce, 28, 44
  Tomato sauce, 75
  Venison sauce, 41
  White sauce, 40
Sausages:
  Sausages and bacon surprise, 76
  Sausages and prune stuffing, 37
  Sausage rolls, 64
  Sausages in barbecue sauce, 74
Savoury cheesecake, 86
Savoury chops, 80
Savoury omelettes, 92
Savoury potato croquettes, 26
Scalloped potatoes, 47
Scallop risotto, 53
Scampi:
  Fried scampi, 25

  Scampi Egyptienne, 25
  Scampi Indienne, 25
  Scampi meunière, 25
  Scampi Provençale, 25
Scone dough, 60, 93
Scotch eggs, corned beef, 90
**Shellfish: see also Crab, lobster,
    prawns, shrimps**
  Shellfish and avocado salad, 30
Sherry sauce, 23
Short crust pastry, 72
Short crust pastry, rich, 72
Short crust pastry, sweet, 72
Shrimps:
  Shrimps and avocado salad, 30
  Shrimp and grapefruit cocktail, 79
Sleigh ride cider cup, 63
Sleigh ride white wine cup, 63
Smoked salmon or trout, 12
Snowden pudding, 28
Sole:
  Sole in white wine, 11
  Sole Normandy, 11
  Sole Veronique, 11
  Sole with mushrooms and
    bamboo shoots, 46
Soufflés:
  Preparing a soufflé dish, 25
  Cheese soufflé, 35
  Cheese soufflé tarts, 25
  Economy soufflé, 35
  Fish soufflé, 34
  Parmesan haddock soufflé, 35
  Peach lemon soufflé, 18
  Spinach soufflé, 35
Soups:
  Brown French onion soup, 39
  Clear tomato soup, 38
  Cream of asparagus soup, 29
  Cream of mushroom soup, 29
  Cream of tomato soup, 36
  Creamy French onion soup, 39
  Greek lemon soup, 22
  Tomato soup, 38
Spaghetti, 75
Spaghetti with tomato and red
  pepper sauce, 52
Spanish sauce, 17
Speedy celery bread, 74
Spiced nuts, 9
Spinach:
  Spinach for eggs Florentine, 43
  Spinach soufflé, 35
Sponge:
  To make, 60
  Sponge flan, 33
  Sponge flan, summer, 33
Steak:
  Cheese-topped steaks, 15
  Crusted savoury steak, 13
  Steaks en croûte, 13
Stew, Chinese lamb, 17
Strawberries:
  Strawberry and lemon cream
    tarts, 76
  Strawberry and peach delight, 62
  Strawberry flan, 83
  Strawberry fluff, 85
  Strawberries in summer flan
    sponge, 32
Stuffed apples, 74
Stuffed boned shoulder of lamb, 16
Stuffed celery, 10
Stuffed chicken legs, 22
Stuffed egg salad, 21
Stuffed peaches, 58
Stuffed pears, 58
Stuffed pigeons, 40
Stuffed turkey legs, 22
Stuffing:
  Chestnut stuffing, 37
  Forcemeat stuffing, 37
  Prune and apple stuffing, 29
  Prune and sausage stuffing, 37
  Raisin and apple stuffing, 17
  Sage and onion stuffing, 17
  Veal stuffing, 37
Sugar plum ring, 65
Sultana cheesecake, 86
Summer sponge flan, 33
Surprise snacks, 65
Sweetbread vol-au-vent, 35
**Sweets: see also Desserts, flans,
    pies, puddings, tarts**
  To serve, 9

Sweet sour sauce, 43
Swiss russe, 81
Swiss steak special, 90
Swiss steak, tomato, 92

Tartare sauce, 28, 44
Tarts and Tartlets:
  Bakewell tart, 72
  Balmoral tartlets, 58
  Cheese soufflé tarts, 25
  Chocolate pear cream tarts, 76
  Cream mincemeat tarts, 57
  Date tartlets, 76
  Dundee orange tart, 67
  Fruit tarts, 45
  Lemon and strawberry cream
    tarts, 76
  Marshmallow prune tarts, 84
  Mexicorn tartlets, 70
  Mincemeat tart, 45
  Mushroom soufflé tarts, 25
Texas three ring rice, 89
Tipsy pork chops, 19
Tomato:
  Celeriac and tomato prelude, 19
  Cheese and tomato slices on
    toast, 77
  Clear tomato soup, 38
  Orange tomato cocktail, 35
  Tomato and Parmesan anchovy
    fingers, 11
  Tomato cheese dip, 72
  Tomato juice cocktail, 34
  Tomato sauce, 75
  Tomato soup, 36, 38
  Tomato Swiss steak, 92
Traditional rich trifle, 31
Trifle:
  Banana rum trifle, 83
  Mandarin trifle, 30
  Pear trifle, 30
  Raspberry trifle, 29
  Rich trifle, 82
  Traditional rich trifle, 31
Trout:
  Smoked trout, 12
Tuna fish darioles, 58
Turkey
  Mushroom stuffed turkey legs, 22
  Roast turkey, 36
  Stuffed turkey legs, 22

Vanilla and apricot bavarois, 17
Veal:
  Escalopes of veal, 26
  Fillets of veal milannaise, 24
  Harlequin rice with veal, 23
  Royal veal, 25
  Veal blanquette with prunes, 26
  Veal cordon bleu, 25
  Veal paprika or goulash, 84
  Veal Portuguese, 27
  Veal roll with prune and apple
    stuffing, 29
  Veal stuffing, 36
  Veal with paprika, 33
  Veal with pâté, 26
Vegetarian vol-au-vent, 35
Venison sauce, 41
Victoria sandwich, 60
Viennese pudding, 22
Vinaigrette (French) dressing, 28
Vol-au-vent:
  Chicken vol-au-vent, 35
  Sweetbread vol-au-vent, 35
  Vegetarian vol-au-vent, 35

Walnut cheese balls, 66
Walnut pie, 21
Walnuts with chicken, 51
Welsh rarebit, 78
White sauce, 40
Wines and wine dishes:
  Choosing wines, 86, 87
  Burgundy beef in red wine, 83
  Claret cup, 63
  Cold Hallowe'en punch, 63
  Sleigh ride cider cup, 63
  Sleigh ride white wine cup, 63
  Sole in white wine, 12
  Vin rosé cup, 63
  Wine casserole of chicken, 83
  White wine cup, 63

York rarebit, 78